Crochet Loom Blooms

Crochet
Loom Blooms

30 Fabulous Crochet Flowers & Projects

Haafner Linssen

Interweave

A QUARTO BOOK

Copyright © 2018 Quarto Publishing plc

Published in North America by
Interweave, an imprint of F+W Media, Inc.
4868 Innovation Drive
Fort Collins, CO 80525
www.interweave.com
All rights reserved.

Conceived, edited, and designed by
Quarto Publishing plc
The Old Brewery
6 Blundell Street
London N7 9BH
www.quartoknows.com

QUAR FLMB

ISBN 978-1-63250-619-1

Editor: Michelle Pickering
Art editor: Jackie Palmer
Designer: Grand Union Design
Photographers: Nicki Dowey,
    Haafner Linssen, and Phil Wilkins
Illustrator: Kuo Kang Chen
Pattern checker: KJ Hay
Editorial assistant: Danielle Watt
Art director: Caroline Guest
Creative director: Moira Clinch
Publisher: Samantha Warrington

Printed in China

10 9 8 7 6 5 4 3 2 1

Contents

About This Book

The book is divided into four chapters, covering essential techniques for before you start making anything, large photographs of all 30 flower motifs to help you select which ones to make, the flower patterns themselves, and then five lovely projects to take your work to another level.

READ ME!

All 30 motifs are made with DK-weight cotton yarn and a size E/4 (3.5mm) crochet hook. Turn to page 36 to find some important information about reading the flower patterns and charts, and the different options for beginning and ending each round of crochet. There is also some essential information about how to adapt the patterns if you want to use a different weight and/or fiber yarn.

Before you begin (pages 10–37)

As much as you might want to dive straight into the tempting flower patterns, it is important to spend a little time in this section of the book, even if you are an experienced crafter. In here, you will find detailed information about the specific flower looms used to make the patterns, followed by clear instructions on how to use the looms. This is followed by a step-by-step guide to all the crochet techniques you will need, and finally some important information about how to read the patterns and charts in the next chapter.

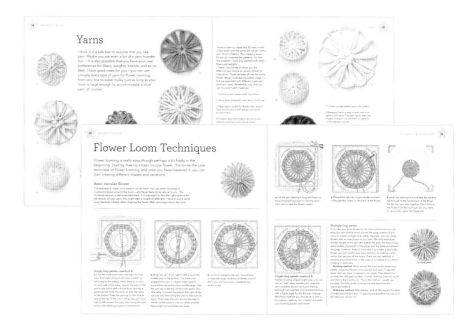

Flower selector (pages 38–47)

Don't know which flower pattern to choose? Turn to this section and spend a little time looking at the stunning large-scale photographs of the flower motifs side-by-side, and soon you will find one leaping out at you. Be inspired and find the flower that is right for you, or get ideas for shapes and colors that work really well together.

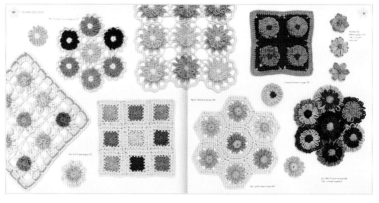

Flower patterns (pages 48–109)

The heart of this book is the 30 flower motif patterns, which are accompanied by charts and beautifully photographed finished examples to help you along your way.

The photographed sample for each pattern includes several flower motifs joined together, either in a row-by-row grid or in a circular formation (as here). For circle and hexagon motifs, you can choose either formation. For all motifs, you can join as many or as few as you like.

The flower motifs are organized according to the finished shape, including the surrounding crochet if any: circles, squares, and hexagons (including a bonus octagon).

Each pattern is graded with a skill level from 1 to 3. Level 1 indicates that a flower is quick-and-easy to make, requiring the most basic looming and crochet skills. Level 2 flowers will take a little longer to make and generally involve a bit more crochet. Level 3 are the most intricate designs, though still easy enough for a beginner to tackle.

The size of the finished flower motif is listed here. The diameter of hexagons is measured from point to point.

A list of the flower looms and any other tools you will need can be found here.

All of the symbols used in the charts are shown here. Check out the loom techniques on pages 18–27 and the crochet techniques on pages 28–33 if you need a reminder on how to perform them.

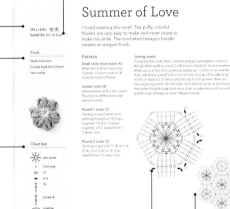

A close-up chart shows one whole motif, plus the outer stitches of several neighboring motifs so that you can clearly see how they are joined. Border stitches are included around the outer edges where appropriate.

This chart shows all of the motifs featured in the photographed example joined together.

Tips and variations are provided to help you get the best results and give you ideas for some simple adaptations.

Projects (pages 110–126)

Loom flowers are beautiful on their own, but what else can you do with them? This chapter provides you with a few ideas, including pattern instructions, charts, and assembly diagrams, for turning your loom flowers into beautiful and unique home and fashion accessories.

Turn to page 127 to learn how to make your own homemade flower looms.

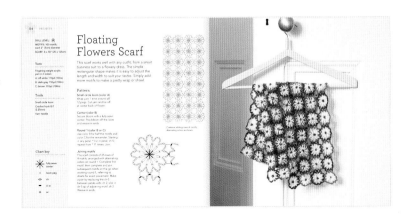

Welcome to My World

A couple of years ago I came across a photograph of a vintage flower loom blanket. It was intricate, delicate, and simply stunning. Until then I only knew flower looming from basic, loose flowers, and I hadn't given much thought to it. But this was a whole new game. I was immediately intrigued and I got myself a flower loom.

I quickly found out that there are surprisingly few sources of information on flower looming, other than how to make a basic flower. But I also discovered that it was a blooming craft in the mid-20th century, when it was used to make all sorts of beautiful items, from dresses and coats to blankets and doilies. After that, flower looming made a bit of a comeback in the 1970s—think big and bold brown and orange flowers—and I guess a lot of us nowadays associate it with that period.

The first thing I ever made with it was the shawl pictured opposite, using both my new loom and my trusted crochet hook. I loved the looming. When I shared the shawl and its pattern on my blog, it turned out that I wasn't the only one who loved loom flowers.

As I started to experiment with my loom, the huge potential of this modest tool became more and more apparent to me, and the idea for a book about this exciting technique began to ripen. It has been an interesting and inspiring journey so far! In this book I'd like to share it with you.

I choose to combine flower looming with crochet, but really, the possibilities are endless. You could integrate the pieces into your weaving, knitting, macramé, or sewing. Also, you can create so much more with a flower loom than "just" flowers, as I hope to show here.

My audacious goal was to take flower looming to a next level. This versatile craft deserves to be part of the basic repertoire of any textile artist.

I hope you will enjoy the book.

Happy flower looming!

Haafner

P.S. Let's connect. I'd really love to see your flower loom work. If you are on social media, spread the loom love by tagging your work #LoomBloom. A beautiful craft is looming, one bloom at a time.

Before You Begin

It's tempting to just grab your loom and go, but before you start your first flower project, it's worth having a read through this chapter. Here, you'll find information about what to expect from the patterns and charts in this book, advice on how to achieve the perfect loom flower, and a handy refresher course in crochet in case you need a quick reminder of the basic techniques.

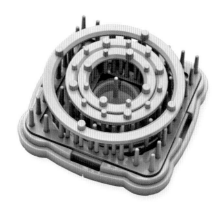

Introducing the Flower Loom

Let me start by saying that flower looming is not difficult to learn, and the small effort required will yield beautiful results. I hope you will enjoy working with your flower loom as much as I do. Happy looming!

Types of loom

There are many types and brands of flower loom available. Some go under other names, such as daisy winder, daisy knitter, or knit wit. Some have pegs, others notches. Some come in fixed sizes and shapes, while others allow you to create your own shapes with loose pegs. They can be made of wood, plastic, cardboard, or metal. They can be purchased or homemade. What they all have in common, however, are the basic principles of flower looming—creating a flower by wrapping yarn around the loom and then sewing the center to secure the petals.

The Hana-Ami loom

The loom used for all the patterns in this book (with just one exception) is the Clover Hana-Ami Flower Loom. It is widely available in craft stores and is easy to purchase online. It comes in a small box containing a base with six loose looms: three circles, two squares, and one hexagon. The box also contains a center peg that is used when you want to wrap the yarn around only part of the

loom, such as when making a quarter circle. There is also a yarn needle for sewing the centers of the flowers to secure them.

Using your flower loom

If you are using the Hana-Ami loom kit, simply choose the loom or looms you wish to use and click them onto the base. You can use a maximum of three circle looms, or other combination of shapes, at the same time.

If you are using another brand or type of loom, the set-up procedure will vary. However, whichever loom you are using, the set-up is always easy, so simply read the instructions that come with your loom.

Once you are set up, it is a good idea to practice the basic techniques of flower looming; many looms come with full instructions, but all the basic loom techniques are explained on the following pages, plus a concise refresher course in crochet techniques. You can then start making any of the patterns in this book.

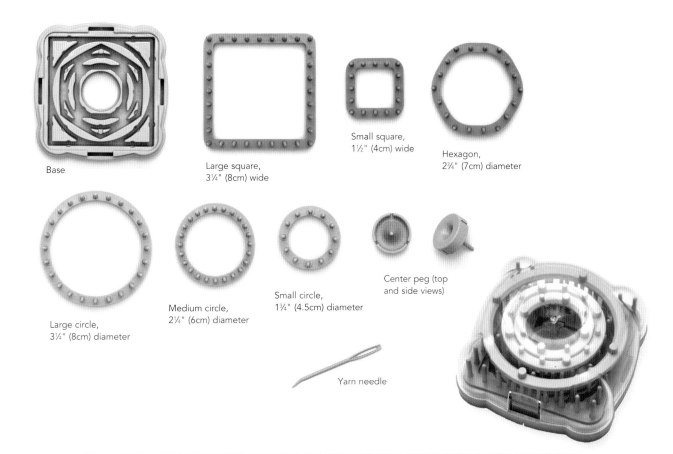

Base

Large square,
3¼" (8cm) wide

Small square,
1½" (4cm) wide

Hexagon,
2¾" (7cm) diameter

Large circle,
3¼" (8cm) diameter

Medium circle,
2¼" (6cm) diameter

Small circle,
1¾" (4.5cm) diameter

Center peg (top
and side views)

Yarn needle

READ THIS FIRST!

• If you are using a different size loom (and/or weight of yarn) from those used in this book, turn to page 37 to find out how to adapt the patterns if necessary.

• Turn to page 127 to find out how to make homemade looms to match the sizes used in this book, or to make any size loom you wish.

• Is it necessary to know how to crochet to use this book? No! Although crochet is a wonderful match for flower looming, see page 34 to discover other techniques for joining the flowers. And, of course, you can always make loose flowers for decoration purposes.

• Part of the challenge when writing the patterns in this book was to create charts and instructions that can be read intuitively and, where applicable, combine well with the language of crochet. You will find an explanation of how to read the patterns and charts on page 36.

Yarns

I think it is a safe bet to assume that you like yarn. Maybe you are even a bit of a yarn hoarder too… It is also possible that you have your own preferences for fibers, weights, brands, and so on. Well, I have good news for you—you can use virtually every type of yarn for flower looming, from very fine to super bulky (just as long as your loom is large enough to accommodate a thick yarn, of course).

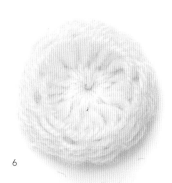

I have chosen to create the 30 main motifs in this book with the same DK-weight cotton yarn (Vinni's Nikkim). This makes it easier for you to compare the patterns. For the five projects, I have also worked with other fibers and weights.

Here, I would like to show you the effect of yarn choice on a loom flower for inspiration. These samples all use the same flower design (overlapping petals, page 21), but are executed with different materials and loom sizes. Remember, too, that you can mix and match materials.

1 Cotton/viscose creates a soft, lacy flower.

2 Hemp gives a beautiful rustic feel to the flower.

3 Paper ribbon is ideal for flowers that need to have a more solid or stiff texture, such as for an adornment.

4 Polyester gives the flower a very shiny look, great for bunting or sprucing up a bag.

5 Subtly multi-toned bamboo/cotton produces a flower with a classical, slightly slubby texture.

6 Fingering-weight acrylic is wonderful for puffy flowers, because the flowers will stay in great shape. I love using this yarn for scarves.

11

14

12

13

10

7 Cotton crochet thread gives a lacy effect.

8 Super soft bamboo/cotton is easy to work with. The best way to keep the flowers in shape is to use them in patterns combined with crochet.

9 Jute is one of my favorite fibers for flower looming. The coarse texture is a wonderful combination with the laciness of loom flowers. Plus, it stays in great shape.

10 Super bulky-weight acrylic yarn is great for super quick and super comfortable throws that stay in great shape after washing.

11 Mercerized cotton is perfect if you are looking for a fiber that is easy to block and stays in good shape afterward. The result is slightly less soft than other cottons, though.

12 Linen makes for a stylish flower.

13 Adding a mercerized cotton center is an easy way to soften the look of a jute flower.

14 T-shirt yarn would be perfect for making a flower loom rug (still on my personal to-do list).

Colors

It almost goes without saying, but your choice of colors is hugely important. The same pattern will look totally different—cheerful, classical, bold, zesty, you name it—depending on the colors. Here, I have made the same flower motif (a scaled-down version of Garden House Grace, page 100) in different color combinations to show you the impact of colors on a pattern.

Monochrome

Bright colors

Soft pastels

Bright pastels

It is not only about the colors themselves, though. It is just as important to decide where to use those colors in your work—and thus how much of each. Would you like a specific color to be the dominant one in a piece, or should it just add a "sparkle" that lets the other colors come out better? And don't neglect colors that you might not automatically be drawn to— sometimes those are the perfect addition for letting other colors take the center stage.

The importance of a color plan is manifest in the series of four flower motifs using black and white—one monochome white motif and three black-and-white samples. Although the colors are the same, by using them in different parts of the pattern—and in the second version with just a hint of black—the four motifs look different.

Black and white

Saturated colors

Variegated yarn

Black and white are always a safe and classical choice, with the dark/light juxtaposition giving any work a geometrical look.

Bright colors are ideal for creating cheery, eye-catching flowers and are always fun to use.

Soft pastels are very soothing and can give your work a vintage look. It is difficult to go wrong with them because they always seem to match. Bright pastels create a different, more zesty result for a refreshing 1950s look.

Saturated colors often seem to add some substance to a work, perfect if you are after a classical look.

The use of variegated yarn can add a certain "organized messiness" to your flower motifs. If combined with monochrome pieces, the effect will be even greater.

PETAL COLOR VARIATIONS

In patterns that use multiple looms, I have often used a different color for each loom, but you can also use more than one color on a single loom. Both of these flowers have multiple-loop petals consisting of four layers of loops made on a single loom (page 19). For the first flower, I alternated the colors per layer (white/gray/white/gray). For the second flower, I alternated the colors per petal.

Flower Loom Techniques

Flower looming is really easy, though perhaps a bit fiddly in the beginning. Start by making a basic circular flower. This forms the core technique of flower looming, and once you have mastered it, you can start creating different shapes and variations.

Basic circular flower

This example is made on a medium circle loom. You can work clockwise or counterclockwise around the loom—whichever feels more natural to you. The clockwise version is demonstrated here. It is important to find the right balance for the tension of your yarn; this might take a couple of attempts. I tend to pull it quite snug, because it helps when shaping the flower after removing it from the loom.

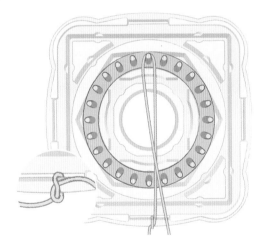

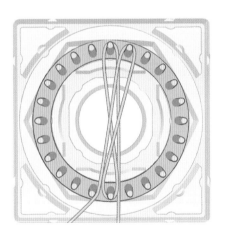

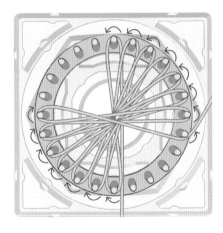

Single-loop petals—method A

1 Click the circle loom onto the base (if it has one). Each type of loom will have a notch or extra peg at the side(s). Here, there is a notch on each side of the base. Attach the end of the yarn to the notch with a loose knot, leaving a generous tail. Hold the loom so that the tail is at the bottom. Take the yarn up to the middle peg at the top of the loom. Wrap the yarn from right to left around the peg, then bring the yarn back to the starting position at the bottom.

2 Wrap the yarn from right to left around the middle peg at the bottom. You have now wrapped the yarn in a figure-eight pattern around the top and bottom middle pegs. Take the yarn up to the top of the loom again. This time wrap it around the peg to the right of the top one and then bring the yarn to the bottom again. Then wrap the yarn around the peg to the left of the bottom one, to create another figure-eight around these two pegs.

3 Continue wrapping the yarn around pairs of opposite pegs, working clockwise around the loom, until you have completed the whole round.

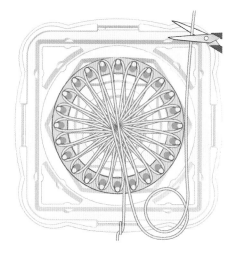

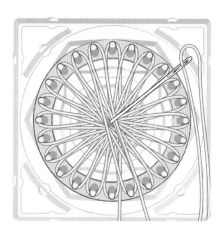

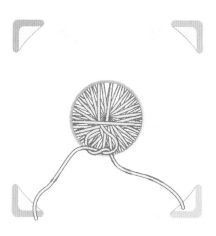

4 Cut the yarn, leaving a long tail (leave an extra long tail if you plan to use the same color yarn to sew the flower center).

5 Thread the tail onto a yarn needle and take it through the center to the back of the flower.

6 Undo the starting knot and take the starting tail through to the center back of the flower. Tie the two yarn tails together. Don't remove the flower from the loom just yet; you need to secure the center first (page 24).

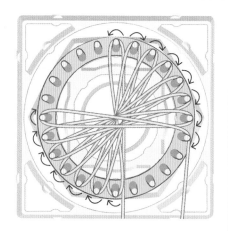

Single-loop petals—method B

Instead of using a figure-eight wrap, you can use an "oval" wrap whereby you wrap the yarn clockwise around each pair of pegs. Although not essential, I recommend starting with a figure-eight for the first pair of pegs. Whichever method you choose, stick with it throughout—getting into a rhythm will make your looming quicker and neater.

Multiple-loop petals

If you like your loom flowers to be more voluminous, you can wrap the yarn several times around the pegs, instead of just once, to create multiple-loop petals. Basically, you can create flowers with as many loops as you wish. The only restrictions are the weight of the yarn (the bulkier the yarn, the fewer loops are possible), the length of the pegs, and the distance between the pegs. However, keep in mind that if you make a very bulky flower, you will need to pay extra attention to making a solid center that secures all the loops. There are two methods of working around the loom in the case of a multiple-loop pattern: rotating or stationary.

Rotating method: Work around the loom as for single-loop petals, wrapping the yarn once around each pair of opposite pegs, until you have completed one round. Then repeat this process the indicated number of times, working a second round and then a third and so on. This is the method I usually use, because I find the result more secure and even than the stationary method.

Stationary method: Alternatively, work all the required number of wraps around each pair of opposite pegs before moving on to the next pair, and so on.

Two-loop petals

Five-loop petals

Using multiple looms

You can combine several sizes of loom to add even more variation to your designs. However, be aware that this is not possible with all looms—very basic ones have just one size.

Double flower

This example is made using medium and small circle looms. Slot both looms onto the base. (If you are using homemade looms, you can tape the small one inside the medium one.) Starting with the medium loom, follow the instructions for making a basic circular flower (page 18). Cut the yarn and take both tails through to the center back as usual. If you have made multiple-loop petals—the sample shown has three-loop petals—gently push the petals tighter to the bottom of the loom to create space for the small petals. Now attach the new color yarn to the side notch. Using the small loom, wrap the yarn to make another set of petals—single-loop petals in the sample. Take both tails through to the back and secure the center (page 24).

Note: If you use the same color for both sizes of loom, you don't have to cut the yarn after completing the petals on the medium loom; simply continue wrapping the yarn around the small loom.

Triple flower

If the type of loom you are using allows it, you can combine three sizes of loom on the base. Begin by wrapping the petals on the largest loom, then the medium loom, and finally the smallest one. Here, the yarn was wrapped three times around the large loom, twice around the medium loom, and once around the small one—you can alter this to your liking, of course.

Petal variations

Here are a few ideas for getting even more creative with your flower looming. The overlapping petals may well be my favorite wrapping technique.

Skipping alternate pegs

You can make fewer petals than there are pegs on the loom. Using a medium circle loom with 24 pegs, for example, simply skip every other peg to create a flower with 12 petals.

TIPS AND TRICKS

• If you find it easier, you can rotate the loom while wrapping the yarn, so that the next pegs to wrap around are always at the top and bottom.

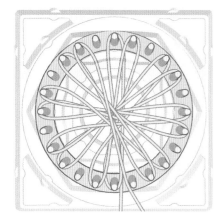

Skipping every third peg

Try skipping pegs in a different pattern. For example, wrap the yarn around the first pair of pegs (top and bottom) and then around the next pair as usual. Then skip the next pair of pegs. Continue looming around two pairs of pegs, skipping the next pair, and so on.

Wider petals

You can create wider petals by wrapping the yarn around two or more pegs at a time, instead of around just one peg. Try wrapping the yarn around three pegs (top and bottom) at a time, as in this example.

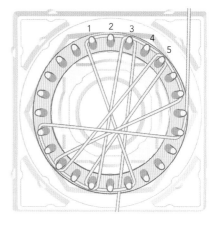

Overlapping petals

Wrap the yarn around two or more pegs at a time, as for making wider petals, but this time include the last peg just wrapped (top and bottom) within the next wrap. For example, wrap the yarn around three pegs at the top (pegs 1, 2, and 3) and then around the opposite three pegs at the bottom. Now take the yarn up to the top again and wrap it around peg 3 plus the next two pegs (pegs 4 and 5), and do the same at the bottom. This pair of petals will partly overlap the first pair and so on, to create a layered effect.

CROCHET FLOWERS

For a lot of flower loom patterns, it is possible to turn them into a crochet pattern. This could be useful if, for instance, you are looking for a portable travel project and don't wish to carry looms around with you. Here is an example:

To start (color A): Make a magic ring, or ch 6 and join with sl st to form a ring.
Round 1 (color A): 12 sc in ring. Join.
Round 2 (color B): Sl st in any sc, [ch 13, sl st in same sc, ch 13, sl st in next sc] 12 times.

Other shapes

Once you have mastered a basic circular flower, working on another shape of loom will be a piece of cake. And the variations don't stop there, because you can also use circle looms to create non-circular flowers.

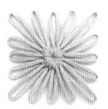

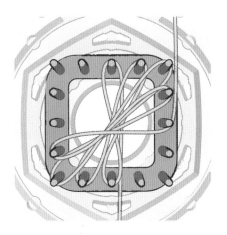

Triangle

You can use either a triangle loom (less commonly available) or a circle loom to make a triangular flower. The latter can be a bit tricky, but if you follow this pattern closely, it should not pose a problem. Click the medium and small circle looms onto the base and attach the yarn to the notch at the bottom. Starting with the middle peg at the top of the medium loom and working clockwise, wrap the yarn around pairs of pegs as follows:

• medium peg to small peg
• small peg to small peg
• small peg to medium peg
• small peg to small peg
• medium peg to small peg
• small peg to small peg

That completes the triangle. You can add more rounds to make it more voluminous following the same pattern. Finish off and secure the center as normal.

Square

Click the square loom onto the base. I find it easiest to start in the exact middle between two corner pegs, wrapping the yarn around the top and bottom middle pegs to start. From there, wrap the yarn around opposite pairs of pegs just as you would when making a circular flower. Each corner peg should be wrapped with the corner peg diagonally opposite—by checking that, you know you are on the right track. Just like a circle, you can go around as many times as you wish. Finish off and secure the center in the same way, too.

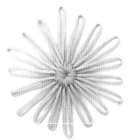

Hexagon

There are also hexagon-shaped looms on the market. Wrap the yarn around the pegs in the same way as you would a circle or square, wrapping the yarn around opposite pairs of pegs as you work around the loom, as many times as you like. Finish off and secure the center as usual.

CROCHET SHAPES

Many of the circular loom flowers in this book are transformed into other shapes by crocheting around them. Examples of hexagons are Spring Bouquet (page 96) and Summer of Love (page 98). Butterfly's Bliss (page 104) is first crocheted into a triangular shape, and then six triangles are joined together to create a larger hexagon.

Quarter circle

If you are using the Hana-Ami loom, click the single center peg into the middle of the base and the medium loom into its slot. If you are using another brand, you can achieve the same effect with two sizes of circle loom by using a peg on the small loom to act like the center peg.

Attach the yarn to the notch at the bottom of the base and then take it up to the top middle peg of the circle loom. Wrap the yarn around the top peg and then around the center peg. Next wrap the yarn around the peg to the right of the top one on the circle loom and then again around the center peg. Continue in this way until you have worked around six or seven pegs on the circle loom, depending on its size. The oval wrapping method (page 19) has been shown here, but you can use the figure-eight method if you prefer.

Cut the yarn, thread it onto a needle, and work it through the middle of all of the loops around the center peg. (This is a bit fiddly because the middle of the loom is closed off by the center peg.) Do the same with the starting tail, then tie the tails together with a knot the keep the center loops together. Leave the flower on the loom and secure the base with a triple backstitch center (page 25).

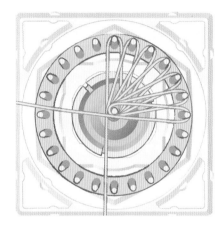

TIPS AND TRICKS

• Some types of yarn can be rather wrinkly, which can adversely affect the results. To prevent that, leave the flower on the loom for a little while after you have sewn the center. Basically, you are blocking the flower on the loom. For an even better result, spray with water and allow to dry completely before removing from the loom.

• Having trouble wrapping the yarn as many times around the loom pegs as indicated in a pattern? Probably the pegs of your flower loom are shorter or you are using a heavier weight yarn. For most (puffy) patterns, it is not a problem if you wrap the yarn once or even twice less around the loom. If it is a pattern using multiple sizes of loom, it is up to you where you want to omit any rounds (on the large, medium, or small loom).

Pompom-esque flowers

You can use one or more circle looms to create a pompom-esque flower—great for dandelions or similar flowers. Simply wrap the yarn around the pegs of the loom as many times as you like; the more rounds, the more pompom-esque the effect. For this sample, the yarn was wrapped five times around the medium loom and twice around the small loom. Secure the center as you normally would; a star center or fully sewn center will create the most fluffy effect (page 24). Gently pop the bloom off the loom. Using scissors, cut all of the loops in two. To make the flower even fluffier, as here, use a yarn needle to "comb" the petals.

Note: If you want to join these flowers together, you will need to keep some of the petal loops intact as joining points (page 34).

TIPS AND TRICKS

• If you are making multiple-loop petals, you can make the flower even more fluffy by wrapping the yarn extra snugly around the pegs. If you leave the flower on the loom for a little while, the effect will be even more pronounced.

Flower centers

Before you remove the flower from the loom, you must always secure the petals at the center first. Otherwise, the work will disintegrate immediately. Once the center is complete, weave in all the yarn tails (including from the petals) on the back of the flower center.

 Fully sewn center

This is a very secure center, suitable for work that will be subject to heavy use, such as baby blankets, throws, or potholders.

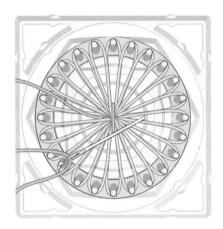

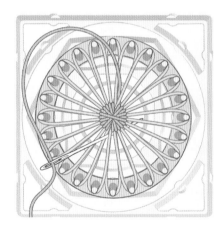

1 Thread a length of yarn onto a yarn needle; the length depends on your yarn and flower size, but you will need at least 18" (45cm) for a 24-petal flower using DK-weight yarn. Leaving a tail at the back, push the needle from the back of the flower through to the front inside a petal loop and then take it down again inside the opposite petal loop. Repeat this process with the next pair of petals. I like to work in a cross formation around the petals, as shown.

2 Continue securing all of the petals in this way, sewing across the center of the flower. Note that you can work the stitches between the petals rather than inside them if you prefer. You can also make a puffy fully sewn center by sewing both inside the petals and between them. For an extra puffy effect (and extra secure bloom), you can work inside and between the petals more than once. Of course, you will need to use a longer thread.

 Star center

This is a secure center, suitable for work that will be subject to use, such as blankets or potholders. You will need at least 24" (60cm) of yarn for a 24-petal flower using DK-weight yarn, though this will vary depending on the yarn and flower size. It is made in the same way as a fully sewn center, except that this time you push the needle through to the front inside (or between) the petals and then take it down again to the back through the center of the flower each time (instead of through the opposite petal). Judge the center by eye to start; after the first few stitches the center will become easier to spot. You can make a puffy (or extra puffy) star center in the same way as a fully sewn center, too.

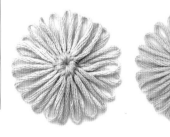

Backstitch center

This center is suitable for decorative items; it will secure your blooms nicely, but is not suitable for anything that will be subject to (heavy) use. Of course, a triple backstitch center will be more secure than a single one, but caution is still advisable. The backstitches can be worked very close to the heart of the flower, or wider if you like that look better. You can also embellish and strengthen a backstitch center by oversewing across the middle of it. Adjust the length of yarn to suit the amount of stitching required for your chosen center.

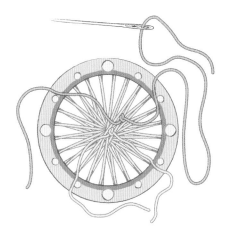

Single backstitch

1 Flip the flower over to the wrong side. Thread a length of yarn onto a yarn needle and carefully take the yarn around all loops of one petal; tie a gentle knot on the reverse to secure the beginning of the stitching.

2 Flip the flower over to the right side. Take the needle under the "knotted" petal and continue under the loops of the next petal. Then bring the needle up to the front of the flower, go back over the second petal, and down again. Pull gently to secure this second petal.

3 Now work the needle under the second petal and continue under the third one. Then bring the needle up, go back over the third petal, and down again. Continue in this way until you have completed the round. You can now weave in the ends and pop the flower off the loom, unless you are making a double or triple backstitch center.

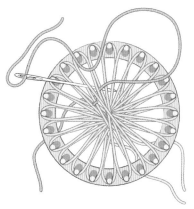

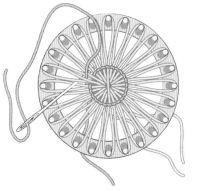

Double backstitch

If you like a more accentuated center, or if you want to secure the petals more tightly, work a second round of backstitch within the first backstitch circle.

Triple backstitch

This is a continuation of the double backstitch center. In principle, it is worked within the circle of double backstitch, but you can also use it to straighten up the wider circle of the first backstitch round—in that case, you work it directly outside that first round.

Oversewn backstitch center

This is a secure center, but be aware that the backstitches can slide a bit with heavy use. Start by sewing a single round of backstitch. Take the yarn through to the back of the flower and then bring it up within the backstitch circle. Now take it over the center of the flower and down again (still within the backstitch circle). Continue like this from one side to the other, oversewing across the whole center of the flower.

❀ Flower bud center

This is the only center that needs its own loom (usually the smallest circle loom), so that means an additional loom to the one(s) being used for the flower petals. It is a fairly secure center, but if you will be using the result of your work a lot, it is advisable to start with a triple backstitch instead of just a single backstitch center.

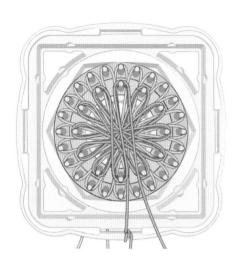

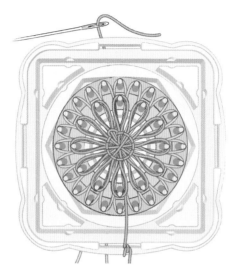

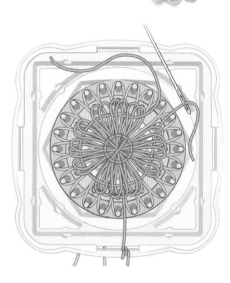

1 Wrap the yarn around the pegs of the small loom in the same way as when making the petals of a flower. You can wrap it once, or twice for a slightly more puffy effect. In this example, the yarn is wrapped once around the medium loom for the petals and twice around the small loom for a puffy flower bud center.

2 Thread the tail from the small loom onto a yarn needle, take it through to the back of the flower, and sew a single backstitch center (page 25).

3 Thread a 10" (25cm) length of yarn onto a yarn needle. Insert it though the loop(s) of the first small petal and then gently pop the threaded petal off the loom. Continue like this with the remaining small petals, one by one, until you are back at the beginning of the round and both tails meet.

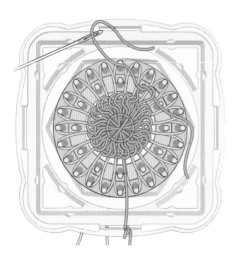

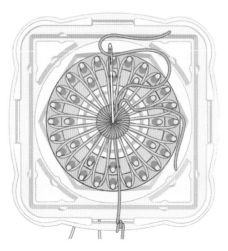

4 Gently pull the tails together, causing the petals to move upward and form a flower bud. Tie the tails together with a knot.

5 Use the yarn needle to thread one tail though the middle of the bud to the back of the flower; the knot will disappear into the center gap. Thread the other tail to the back via the side of the bud to complete the center.

Back of flower centers

Depending on the type of project you are making, you may want the back of your flower centers to look just as neat as the front. I find the easiest way to achieve this is to finish the back with a modified oversewn or fully sewn back center. A big bonus is that this secures the petals even tighter, so it is especially recommended for projects like blankets.

With a standard oversewn or fully sewn center, you take the sewing yarn from the back to the front to the back again, but since you don't want to mess up the center you have made on the front of the flower, this time you should take the sewing yarn through the middle layer of the center, from side to side, instead of pushing the needle all the way to the front.

If you are finishing the center back of the flower in this way, make sure to leave an extra long tail when making the front center. This way, you only have to use one thread to make both the front and back centers. Another way to prettify the back is to add an embellishment, such as a vintage button.

Embellishments

After securing the center of the flower with one of the sewn flower center methods, you can add all kinds of embellishments to them. Here are a few examples to get you started.

Button

A simple and much-used method for prettifying a loom flower is to sew a button on the center. I recommend securing the bloom with a fairly flat sewn center underneath. This example is secured with a star center and topped with a vintage fabric button.

Sequins

You could use one large sequin or lots of small ones. This sample was finished with a backstitch center and then the sequins were sewn on top with embroidery thread.

Crochet

Crochet a small circle and sew it onto the flower center—simple yet effective. The petals of this flower were secured with a backstitch center before adding the crocheted circle.

TIPS AND TRICKS

• Opposite loops of a flower are like communicating vessels—if you pull one too hard, it will enlarge/stick out and the opposite one will correspondingly shrink. So handle your flowers with care when sewing the centers and joining flowers together. Also, the better you secure the center, the less this issue will occur.

• Mix and match! The patterns in this book are great for combining and adapting. For example, if you like a particular flower but would prefer another center, simply finish your flower with a different center. That way, you can make almost endless combinations.

Crochet Techniques

Even experienced crocheters need their memories jogged from time to time. Whether you are a beginner or have been crocheting for years, these pages provide a handy reference guide to the key stitches and techniques.

Basic stitches

All crochet stitches are based on a loop of yarn pulled through another loop by a hook, repeated a different number of times to create stitches of different heights.

Slip knot

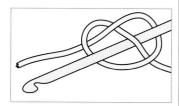

1 Make a loop of yarn and insert the crochet hook.

2 Gently pull on the short and long ends of yarn while holding the hook to create a slip knot.

○ Chain stitch (ch)

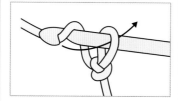

1 Make a slip knot as shown left. Wrap the yarn over the hook (or catch it with the hook) and pull it through the loop on the hook to make a new loop. One chain stitch (ch) made.

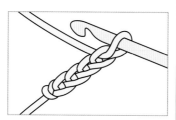

2 Repeat step 1 as required, moving your left hand every few stitches to hold the chain just below the hook.

● Slip stitch (sl st)

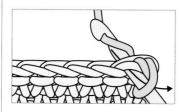

1 Insert the hook in the designated stitch (or space), wrap the yarn over the hook, and pull a new loop through both the work and the loop on the hook. One slip stitch (sl st) made.

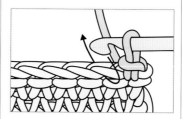

2 Repeat step 1 in each stitch to the end to complete one row of slip stitches.

+ Single crochet (sc)

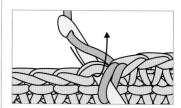

1 Insert the hook in the designated stitch (or space), wrap the yarn over the hook, and pull a new loop through the work only.

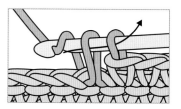

2 Wrap the yarn over the hook and pull a new loop through both loops on the hook.

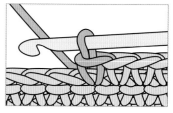

3 One loop remains on the hook. One single crochet stitch (sc) made. Repeat steps 1–2 in each stitch to the end to complete one row of single crochet stitches.

Half double crochet (hdc)

1 Wrap the yarn over the hook and insert the hook in the designated stitch (or space).

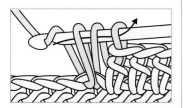

2 Pull a new loop through the work. You now have three loops on the hook. Wrap the yarn over the hook again. Pull through all three loops on the hook.

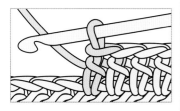

3 One loop remains on the hook. One half double crochet stitch (hdc) made. Repeat steps 1–2 in each stitch to the end to complete one row of half double crochet stitches.

Double crochet (dc)

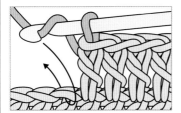

1 Wrap the yarn over the hook and insert the hook in the designated stitch (or space).

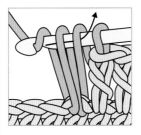

2 Pull a new loop through the work to make three loops on the hook. Wrap the yarn over the hook again. Pull a new loop through the first two loops on the hook.

3 Two loops remain on the hook. Wrap the yarn over the hook again. Pull a new loop through both loops on the hook.

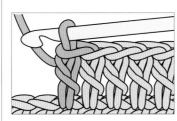

4 One loop remains on the hook. One double crochet stitch (dc) made. Repeat steps 1–3 in each stitch to the end to complete one row of double crochet stitches.

Treble crochet (tr)

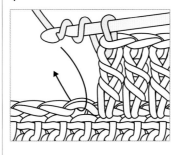

1 Wrap the yarn twice over the hook and insert the hook in the designated stitch (or space).

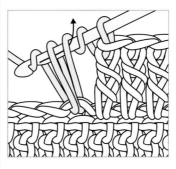

2 Pull a new loop through the work. You now have four loops on the hook. Wrap the yarn over the hook again and pull through the first two loops.

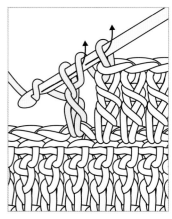

3 Three loops remain on the hook. Wrap the yarn over the hook and pull through the first two loops. Two loops remain on the hook. Wrap the yarn over again and pull through the two remaining loops.

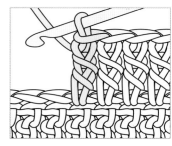

4 One loop remains on the hook. One treble crochet stitch (tr) made. Repeat steps 1–3 in each stitch to the end to complete one row of treble crochet stitches.

Working into one loop only

The hook is usually inserted under both loops at the top of a stitch, but if it is inserted under just one loop, the empty loop creates a ridge on the front or back of the fabric. A few of the patterns in this book use the back loops only for some stitches; in all cases, "back loop" refers to the loop nearest the wrong side of the work.

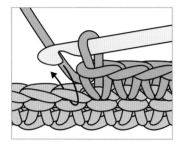

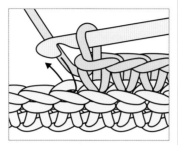

⌣ **Front loop only**
If the hook is inserted under the front loop only, the empty back loop will show as a ridge on the other side of the work.

⌢ **Back loop only**
If the hook is inserted under the back loop only, the empty front loop creates a ridge on the side of the work facing you.

Decreases and clusters

Several stitches may be joined together at the top to decrease the total number of stitches. This can be denoted in the pattern using the abbreviation "tog" along with the type and number of stitches—for example, dc3tog. Clusters are several stitches worked in the same place and joined together at the top—for example, 3-dc cluster. The method of joining the stitches together at

the top is the same for both. To do this, work each stitch to be joined up to (but not including) the last "yarn over and pull through." One loop from each stitch will remain on the hook, plus the loop from the previous stitch. Yarn over once more and then pull a loop through all the loops on the hook to complete. Any number of any type of stitch can be worked together in a similar way.

Working in rounds

Most of the time in this book, the first round of crochet stitches is worked into the petals of the loom flower, but occasionally you will need to start a crochet round from scratch. You can do this by working outward from a ring of chain stitches or from a magic ring.

Chain ring

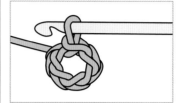

1 Make a short length of chain stitches as specified in the pattern. Join the chains into a ring by working a slip stitch into the first chain.

2 Inserting the hook into the space at the center of the ring each time, work the first round of crochet stitches as instructed in the pattern.

ⓔ Magic ring

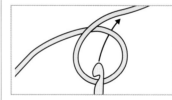

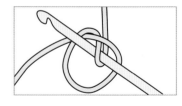

1 Start by making a loop of yarn and then insert the hook into the loop.

2 Catch the working yarn (the end coming from the ball) with the hook and pull it through the loop.

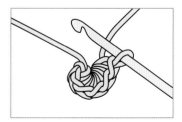

3 Crochet the desired number of stitches into the center of the loop.

4 Pull the short yarn end to close the center of the magic ring.

Standing stitches

Chain stitches are usually used to form the first stitch of a new round. However, a standing stitch is a great way to start a round without using chains and is my preferred method (see page 36 for more information).

Standing single crochet

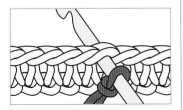

1 Make a slip knot on the hook and then insert the hook in the indicated stitch (or space).

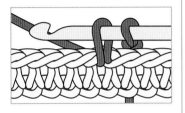

2 From here it is just like finishing a regular sc—yarn over, pull up a loop, yarn over, and pull through both loops on the hook.

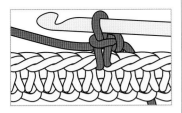

3 The stitch will have a little bump on the back (the initial slip knot). If you like, you can unravel this bump after completing the round; the stitch will stay secure.

Standing double crochet—method A

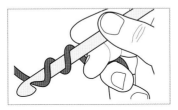

1 Wrap the yarn around the hook twice and secure these loops with a finger (this part can be a bit fiddly at first, but after a few times you will get the hang of it).

2 Insert the hook in the indicated stitch (or space) and pull up a loop.

3 From here it is like finishing a regular dc—[yarn over and pull through two loops] twice.

Standing double crochet—method B

1 Make a slip knot on the hook. (As with a standing sc, you can unravel the slip knot after completing the round if you wish; the stitch will stay secure.)

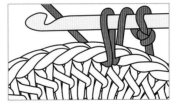

2 Yarn over and insert the hook in the indicated stitch (or space). Pull up a loop.

3 From here it is like finishing a regular dc—[yarn over and pull through two loops] twice.

Variations of the standing double crochet

If you have mastered the standing double crochet, it is easy to make variations. For instance:

Standing dc cluster

If a pattern calls for a dc cluster as the first stitch of a round, start by making a standing double crochet, but don't finish it (just like you would not finish a regular dc when working a cluster). Now work the remaining stitches of the cluster and finish in the usual way.

Standing hdc or standing tr

For a standing hdc, follow steps 1–2 of the standing dc (either method) and then yarn over and pull through all three loops on the hook. If a pattern calls for a treble (tr) as the first stitch of a round, use the same technique as for the standing dc, but wrap the yarn over the hook three times (instead of two).

Joining rounds

Throughout the patterns in this book, you will see the instruction "join" at the end of a round. The most common way to join a round of crochet is with a slip stitch. However, the other option you have is to close the round using a yarn needle. This is my preferred method because it gives an invisible join.

For some patterns the slip stitch join is absolutely fine—it will have less impact on a lacy pattern, for example. For other patterns, however—in general the more solid ones—a slip stitch will create a visible, less attractive join. For those patterns, it really will create a much prettier, more polished result if you use a yarn needle to create a seamless join. Give both a try and then use whichever method you prefer for joining your rounds.

Joining with a slip stitch

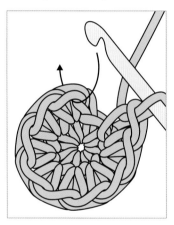 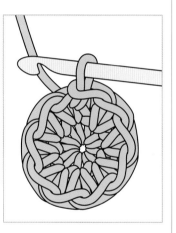

1 When you reach the end of the round, work a slip stitch into the top of the very first stitch of the round.

2 Here is the result. Remember that the slip stitch does not count as a stitch when working the next round.

Joining with a yarn needle

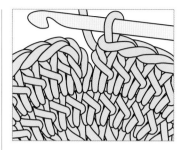 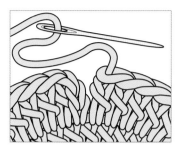

1 Complete the last stitch of the round. Cut the yarn, leaving a tail of about 4" (10cm).

2 Remove the hook from the last loop and draw the tail through the loop. Thread the tail onto a yarn needle.

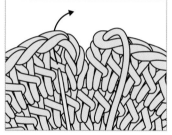 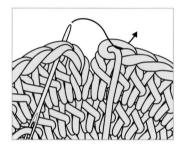

3 Insert the needle under both strands of the top V-shaped loop to the left of the first stitch (or starting chain). Draw the yarn all the way through.

4 Insert the needle, from front to back, between the strands of the V-shaped loop at the top of the last stitch you worked (at the end of the round).

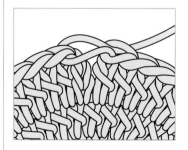 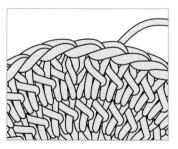

5 Pull the yarn through.

6 Adjust the tension of the yarn until the join is seamless. Weave in the end.

Fastening off and weaving in ends

It is very easy to fasten off yarn when you have finished a piece of crochet, but do not cut the yarn too close to the work because you need enough yarn to weave in the end. It is important to weave in yarn ends securely so that they do not unravel. Do this as neatly as possible so that the woven yarn does not show through on the front of the work.

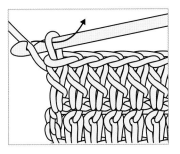 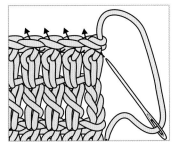 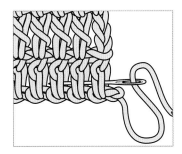

Fastening off

To fasten off the yarn securely, work one chain and then cut the yarn at least 4" (10cm) away from the work. Pull the tail through the loop on the hook and tighten it gently.

Weaving in ends

To weave in a yarn end along the top or lower edge of a piece of crochet, start by threading the end onto a yarn needle. Take the needle through several stitches on the wrong side of the crochet, working stitch by stitch. Trim the remaining yarn. When crocheting the flower motifs, try to weave the ends through the lower stitches because this will make the ends less visible.

Blocking

I strongly recommend that you block your finished work. I would even go so far as to say that for most pieces it is essential, because it makes the design really come out. Keep in mind that loom blooms can be a bit fragile, so handle with care.

Use a clean, soft surface, such as a folded towel, blanket, or foam mattress, as a base. It needs to be of some substance so you can use pins. Put the work on top and gently shape it. A fluffy flower might need some fluffing up, while others need more stretching, depending on the design.

Pin the flower in (or near) the center and then pin the individual petals. It works best if you pin two pairs of opposite petals first (and thus create a cross shape) and then pin the remaining petals. Remember that opposite petals are directly connected with each other, so if you stretch one petal too strongly, it could shorten the opposite petal. This depends on the type of yarn and flower center, but if it happens, gently pull the short one back to its original length.

Pin the crochet section (if any) in the same way, pinning opposite sides or corners at a time. If blocking a piece that consists of several joined flower motifs, pin the middle flower first and work outward from there.

Lightly spray the pinned work with water. Leave it for at least a couple of hours (up to a day). You might want to spray it once or twice more, depending on how much shaping the work needs. When completely dry, gently remove the pins. If there are loose petals on the design, fluff them up if necessary.

For individual loom flowers with no crochet, you can block them on the loom rather than pin them out, but this will slow you down if you want to make more flowers but only have one loom.

Joining Methods

There are a couple of decisions to be made when it comes to joining your loom flowers and motifs, and the method you choose will have a huge impact on the final look of your work.

Joining on the loom

This gives a very lacy look, but note that the loose connection makes it more difficult for the flowers to keep their shape. Complete the first flower, including the center, and pop it off the loom. When making the second flower, pull the working yarn through the desired petal of the first flower to join and then continue wrapping around the pegs of the second flower as usual. You can join as many petals as you wish.

Knots

Easy peasy. Turn the flowers over to the wrong side and use a length of yarn to tie the desired petals together with a double knot. This is a secure way of joining and the flowers stay well in place. Take one tail from the knot down to the center back of each joined flower and weave in.

ORDER OF JOINING

You can join your flower motifs in any order you like, but for consistency all the charts in this book show the following order:

• Grid formation: starting at top-left motif, join from left to right across each row, from top to bottom.

• Circular formation: starting at middle motif, join upper-right motif and then continue clockwise around, finishing with top motif.

• Remember that any circle or hexagon motif can be joined in either formation—the choice is yours.

Join all loops?

If you have flowers with multiple-loop petals, this simple decision can change the finished result considerably. These identical flower motifs are made by wrapping the yarn three times around each peg on the loom, followed by a circle of crochet stitches, but there is one minor difference—with a huge impact. On the first motif, the crochet stitches are worked through the lowest loop only, leaving the top two loops of each petal loose. On the second motif, the crochet stitches are worked through all three loops of each petal. The results look very different. This is something to keep in mind when you start designing your own motifs, or if you would like to make a simple change to one of the patterns in this book.

Joining crochet motifs

Loom flowers that are set within a framework of crochet stitches can be joined on the go while working the final round of crochet, or they can be joined together afterward with a crochet or sewn seam.

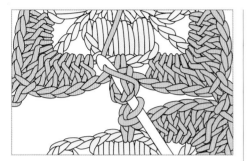

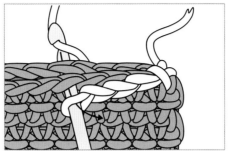

Joining on the go

Complete the first motif, then complete and join subsequent motifs on the go when working the final round. Most of the joins in this book are made by replacing a chain stitch (usually the middle chain of a group of chain stitches) with a slip stitch into the corresponding chain space of the adjoining motif. To do this, with the right side of the first motif facing up, insert the hook from below through the chain space and work a slip stitch. Continue the final round of the second motif as usual. When three or four motifs meet together, insert the hook into the chain space of the motif diagonally opposite, or whichever motif you think gives the neatest result. In the case of three hexagons adjoining, you can join the third motif by working the slip stitch through the space between the join of the first two motifs.

Crochet seam

Complete all the motifs before joining. With right sides together, work a row of slip stitch (shown here) or single crochet through both motifs together. You can work the stitches through both loops of each pair of stitches or just through the back (wrong-side) loops for a less bulky seam.

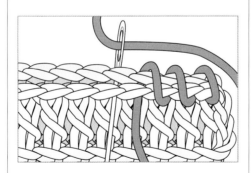

Whipstitch seam

Complete all the motifs before joining. Using a yarn needle and with right sides together, sew through the loops of the first pair of stitches, then take the needle over the edge of the work and sew through the next two stitches and so on. You can sew through both loops of each pair of stitches or just through the back (wrong-side) loops for a less bulky seam.

Minor variations, big difference

Both of these loom flowers are exactly the same, but minor variations in the crochet produce very different results. In the first example, 1 sc has been worked into each of the 24 petal loops, with 1 ch separating each sc. In the second example, 1 sc has been worked into 2 petal loops together, with 5 ch separating each sc. The motifs are joined on the go by replacing the ch-1 or the middle ch of the ch-5 with a slip stitch into the adjoining motif, with three joins between the motifs.

Reading the Patterns

The information and tips here will help you to get a good understanding of the patterns, and I recommend that you read them before picking up your loom and hook.

Rounds of crochet stitches are shown in alternating shades of gray (with just a couple of exceptions when color is used for clarity).

The flower petals and centers—anything that is worked on the loom—are shown in color.

Stitches used to join the flower motifs are highlighted in solid black so that they stand out clearly.

One petal can consist of more than one loop. The written pattern specifies the number of loops to wrap around each loom peg to form a petal.

A key to all of the chart symbols is listed beside each pattern.

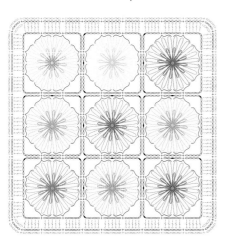

The close-up chart shows one complete flower motif—the top-left motif on patterns that are joined in a grid formation, or the center motif on patterns that are joined in a circular formation—plus the outer rounds of two or three adjoining motifs and any border stitches. The multi-motif chart shows how all the motifs fit together (see also Order of Joining, page 34).

ABBREVIATIONS

ch	chain
sl st	slip stitch
sc	single crochet
hdc	half double crochet
dc	double crochet
tr	treble crochet
sp(s)	space(s)
st(s)	stitch(es)
yo	yarn over

Starting a new round

You have two options for how to start each new round of crochet. My preferred method is to use a standing stitch (page 31), because it gives a seamless start to the round. The other, more common, option is to use chain stitches to count as the first stitch of the round. If you prefer to use chains, I recommend making one chain in place of a half double crochet, and two chains in place of a double crochet. For single crochet, work one chain followed by a single crochet stitch (note that the chain is in addition to the first single crochet stitch of the round; it does not replace it). I also prefer to start each new round in a different place, rather than directly on top of the first stitch of the previous round, in order to blend in more seamlessly. For patterns worked in rows, I recommend starting each row with chains rather than standing stitches. Starting with chains is less noticeable when working in rows and will also be more durable.

Joining at the end of a round

The patterns simply instruct you to "join" at the end of the round. Again, you have two options. You can join the last stitch to the first stitch with a slip stitch, which is the most common method. Or you can use a yarn needle to join the two stitches together, which is my preferred method because it produces an invisible join. See page 32 for how to do both.

Size matters—a lot

Usually with a crochet pattern, you can easily size the pattern up or down by using a different weight of yarn and a matching size of hook. With the patterns in this book, it is slightly different, so please read this carefully.

What is different is that the flower looms come in fixed sizes, which means that if you use a thinner or more voluminous yarn than in my sample, you can alter the size of the hook to match the yarn weight, but the size of the loom remains the same. Let me show you what I mean on the basis of one pattern executed in three different yarns. All of these are made on the same medium circle loom by wrapping the yarn once around each of the 24 pegs, and by working each single crochet stitch of round 1 into two petals (2 loops) together.

You see? In order to make the pattern work using the same size loom but a different weight and/or fiber yarn, you will have to adapt the number of crochet stitches accordingly. This means that if you wish to use a different yarn weight, fiber, or hook, the patterns in this book will give you general guidance, but you may have to trust your skills and add or omit a couple of stitches to keep your work flat and prevent it from either cupping or ruffling (page 33). You can also experiment with sizing your loom up or down (page 127) or making the flower using crochet petals (page 21).

Medium motif

This is the weight of yarn used to make all 30 motifs in this book.

Yarn: DK-weight cotton
Hook: E/4 (3.5mm)

Round 1: Starting in any pair of petals: *[1 sc in 2 petals together, ch 1] twice, [1 sc, ch 2, 1 sc] in next 2 petals together, ch 1; repeat from * 3 times. Join.
Round 2: Starting in any corner ch-2 sp: *[2 dc, ch 2, 2 dc] in ch-2 sp, [1 dc in next sc, 1 dc in next ch-1 sp] 3 times, 1 dc in next sc; repeat from * 3 times. Join.

Fine motif

A thinner yarn is used here, so more stitches are needed to complete each round.

Yarn: Fingering-weight crochet cotton
Hook: Steel 12 (1mm)

Round 1: Starting in any pair of petals: *[1 sc in 2 petals together, ch 4] twice, [1 sc, ch 4, 1 sc] in next 2 petals together, ch 4; repeat from * 3 times. Join.
Round 2: Starting in any corner ch-4 sp: *[3 dc, ch 2, 3 dc] in ch-4 sp, [1 dc in next sc, 5 dc in next ch-4 sp] 3 times, 1 dc in next sc; repeat from * 3 times. Join.

Bulky motif

A thicker yarn is used here, so fewer stitches are needed to complete each round.

Yarn: Bulky-weight cotton/acrylic
Hook: K/10½ (6.5mm)

Round 1: Starting in any pair of petals: *[1 sc in 2 petals together] twice, [1 sc, ch 3, 1 sc] in next 2 petals together; repeat from * 3 times. Join.
Round 2: Starting in any corner ch-3 sp: *[2 dc, ch 2, 2 dc] in ch-3 sp, 1 dc in each of next 4 sc; repeat from * 3 times. Join.

Flower Selector

This chapter showcases all 30 flower motifs, shown at 45% actual size. Look through the selector to help you choose the design you want to make. Motifs that don't require any crochet are indicated, plus you can of course make any of the individual loom flowers and simply omit the crochet framework. Each motif is labeled with the page number where you will find the written pattern and charts, so simply select your design, turn to the relevant page, and begin looming.

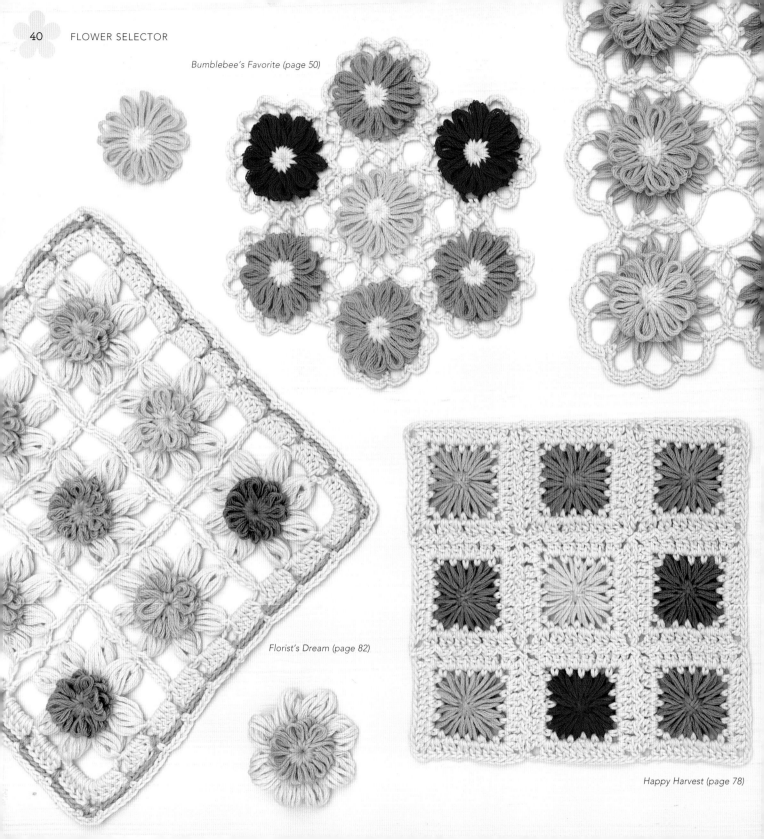

Bumblebee's Favorite (page 50)

Florist's Dream (page 82)

Happy Harvest (page 78)

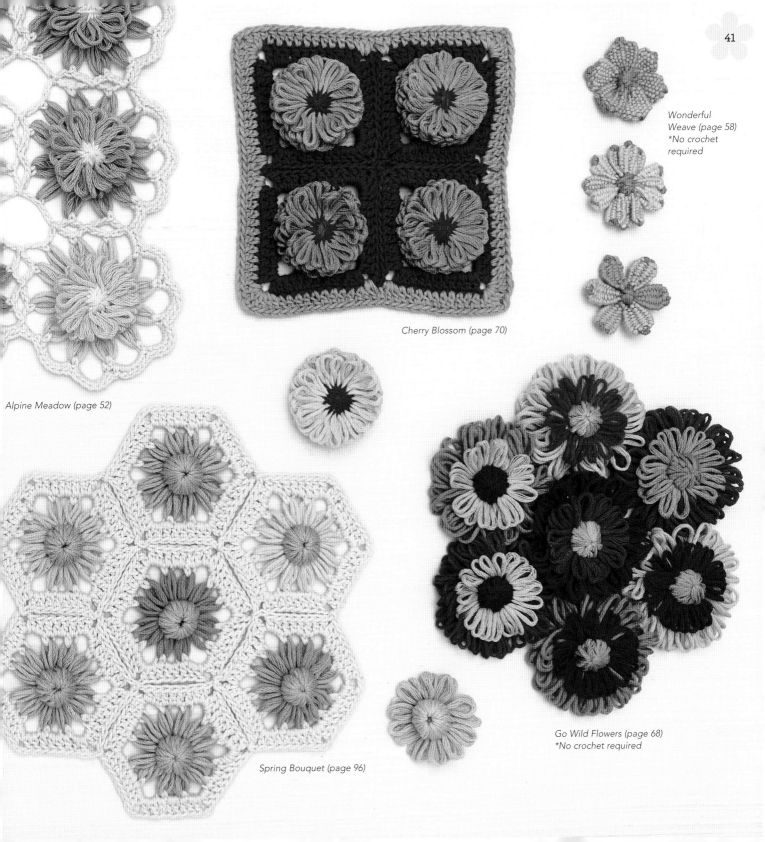

Wonderful
Weave (page 58)
*No crochet
required

Cherry Blossom (page 70)

Alpine Meadow (page 52)

Go Wild Flowers (page 68)
*No crochet required

Spring Bouquet (page 96)

Garden House Grace (page 100)

Go Green (page 66)

Butterfly's Bliss (page 104)

What You Sow (page 94)

Stockholm Gardens (page 72)

Flower Fair (page 90)

The Conservatory (page 92)

Formal Flower Bed (page 60)

Doting on Dots (page 84)

My Little Flower Patch (page 106)
*No crochet required

Fall Wedding Bouquet (page 80)

Wonderful Weave (page 58)
*No crochet required

Bucolic Blossom (page 86)

Summer of Love (page 98)

Pretty Posy (page 74)

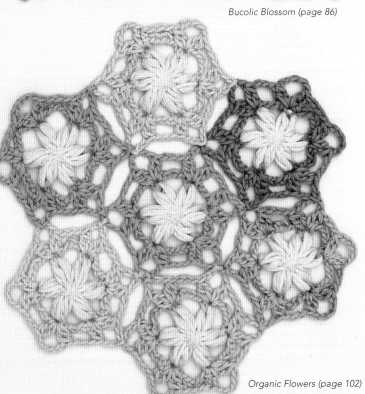

Organic Flowers (page 102)

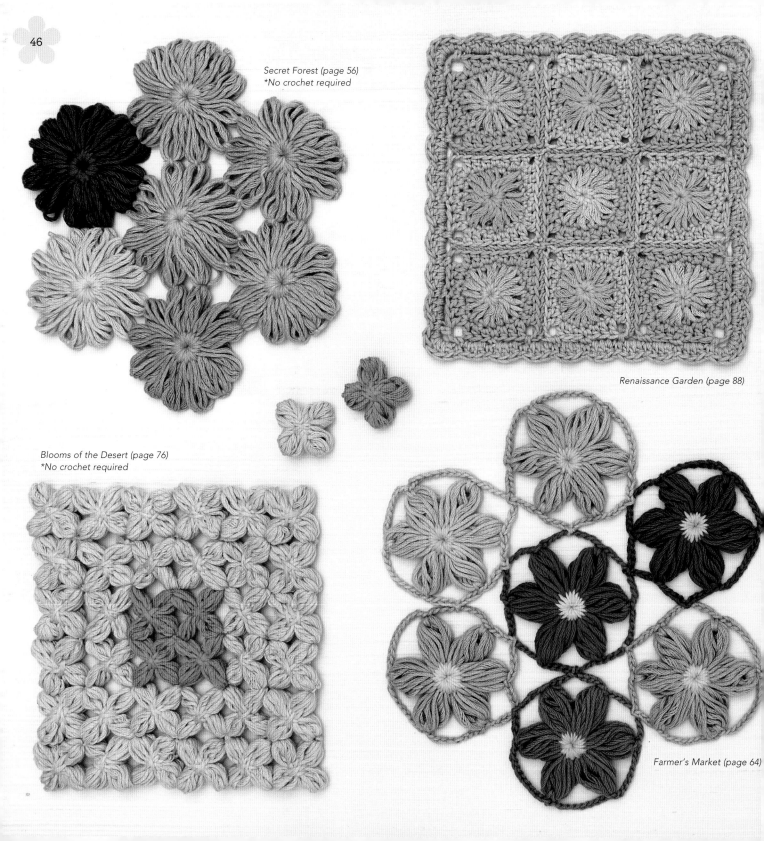

46

Secret Forest (page 56)
*No crochet required

Renaissance Garden (page 88)

Blooms of the Desert (page 76)
*No crochet required

Farmer's Market (page 64)

*Stockholm Gardens
(page 72)*

Delightful Daisies (page 54)

Regent's Park (page 108)

Tales From My Garden (page 62)

Flower Patterns

In this chapter you will find 30 flower loom patterns for you to try out, organized by the shape of the complete motif, including the surrounding crochet if any: circles, squares, and hexagons. They range from the simplest designs, using only one flower loom and the most basic crochet stitches, to more intricate patterns with layers of multiple-loop petals and a greater range of crochet stitches. Pages 36–37 offer useful guidance on reading the patterns, so be sure to give them a read before you begin.

Bumblebee's Favorite

This delightful yet uncomplicated motif is not only this little critter's favorite, but also the quintessential flower loom pattern.

SKILL LEVEL:

DIAMETER: 2¾" (7cm)

Tools

Medium circle loom

Crochet hook E/4 (3.5mm)

Yarn needle

Chart key

 puffy star center

o loom peg

⬭ ch

⬬ sl st

+ sc

Pattern

Medium circle loom (color A)

Wrap yarn 3 times around 12 pegs, skipping every other peg. Cut yarn and tie off at center back of flower.

Center (color B)

Secure bloom with a puffy star center. Pop bloom off the loom and weave in ends.

Round 1 (color B)

Starting in any petal and working through lowest loop only (2 loops remain loose): *1 sc in petal, ch 5; repeat from * 11 times. Join.

Joining motifs

Complete first motif, then complete and join subsequent motifs on the go when working round 1, referring to charts for exact placement. Make a join by replacing the ch-5 between petals with: ch 2, sl st in ch-5 sp of adjoining motif, ch 2. Weave in ends.

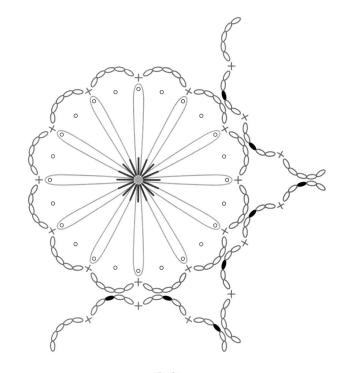

Shown at 90% actual size

Alpine Meadow

These light, airy flowers are like a breath of fresh air and would make a lovely gift. The pattern uses only two circle looms and is fairly quick and easy.

SKILL LEVEL:

DIAMETER: 3¼" (8.5cm)

Tools

Large circle loom

Medium circle loom

Crochet hook E/4 (3.5mm)

Yarn needle

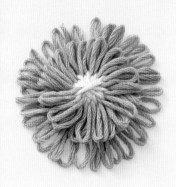

Chart key

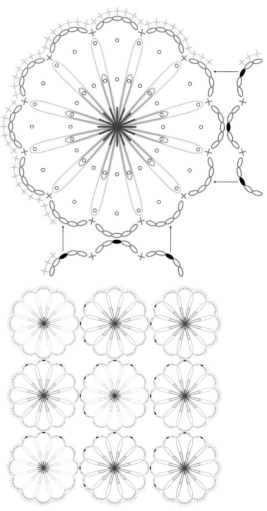

puffy fully
sewn center

○   loom peg

⬭   ch

⬬   sl st

✛   sc

Pattern

Large circle loom (color A)
Wrap yarn 3 times around 12 pegs, skipping every other peg. Do not cut yarn.

Medium circle loom (color A)
Wrap yarn 3 times around 12 pegs, skipping every other peg. Cut yarn and tie off at center back of flower.

Center (color B)
Secure bloom with a puffy fully sewn center. Pop bloom off the loom and weave in ends.

Round 1 (color B)
Starting in any large petal and working through all 3 loops together: *1 sc in petal, ch 5; repeat from * 11 times. Join.

Joining motifs
Complete first motif, then complete and join subsequent motifs on the go when working round 1, referring to charts for exact placement. Make a join by replacing the ch-5 between petals with: ch 2, sl st in ch-5 sp of adjoining motif, ch 2. Weave in ends.

Border (color B)
The simple single crochet border gives a bit of structure to the outer parts of this lacy pattern, but you can omit it if you prefer. Work 7 sc in every ch-5 sp and 3 sc in every ch-2 sp (the spaces where two blooms are joined). Join. Weave in ends.

Shown at 70% actual size

Delightful Daisies

SKILL LEVEL: ✿✿
DIAMETER: 2⅜" (6cm)

Who doesn't love a daisy? This pattern captures the effortless charm of the daisy perfectly. Get out your embroidery needle and go for it.

Tools

Medium circle loom

Crochet hook E/4 (3.5mm)

Yarn needle

Sharp embroidery needle

Pattern

Medium circle loom (color A)
Wrap yarn 2 times around all 24 pegs. Cut yarn and tie off at center back of flower.

Center (color B)
Secure bloom with a backstitch center. Using embroidery needle and working from the backstitch circle toward the middle, fill the center with small running stitches, pushing the needle up and down through the flower. Use a sharp needle for this, because the fabric will get quite dense, especially toward the middle. Pop bloom off the loom and weave in ends.

Round 1 (color C)
Starting in any petal and working through lowest loop only (1 loop remains loose): *1 sc in petal, ch 1; repeat from * 23 times. Join.

Joining motifs
Complete first motif, then complete and join subsequent motifs on the go when working round 1, referring to charts for exact placement. Make a join by replacing the ch-1 between petals with: sl st in ch-1 sp of adjoining motif. Weave in ends.

Chart key

 backstitch center filled with running stitch

○ loom peg

⬯ ch

⬮ sl st

+ sc

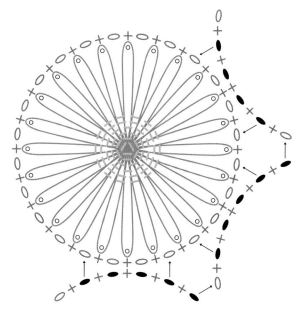

Shown at 90% actual size

VARIATION

Why not make a daisy chain with the loose flowers?
Simply lace your daisies together or crochet a simple
string of chain stitches. It would make a lovely hair
accessory or cute little bunting.

Secret Forest

Deep in the forest, you will find an enchanting open space where these mysterious flowers bloom—or you can create them yourself. These large, puffy blooms are joined by a simple knot.

SKILL LEVEL:

DIAMETER: 2¾" (7cm)

Tools

Large circle loom

Yarn needle

Stitch markers

Chart key

puffy star center

o   loom peg

*   knot

⌢   together

Pattern

Large circle loom
(color A throughout)

Wrap yarn 3 times around all 24 pegs. Cut yarn, leaving an extra long tail, and tie off at center back of flower.

Center

Using long tail, secure bloom with a puffy star center. Pop bloom off the loom and weave in ends.

Step 1

Using a stitch marker, secure the first 2 petals (6 loops) together so that they form a large puffy petal. Repeat to make 12 puffy petals in total.

Step 2

Turn flower over to wrong side. Thread a 4" (10cm) length of yarn through all 6 loops of each puffy petal and tie a double knot to secure. Take yarn tails to center back of bloom and weave in ends.

Joining motifs

Complete first motif, then complete and join subsequent motifs on the go when working step 2, referring to charts for exact placement. Make a join by tying the yarn through a puffy petal of the adjoining motif at the same time as the working motif. Weave in ends.

Shown at 90% actual size

Wonderful Weave

SKILL LEVEL: ❀ ❀ ❀
DIAMETER: 2" (5cm)

Tools

Medium circle loom

Yarn needle (extra long)

Use the flower loom as a tiny weaving loom to create these delicate woven flowers and open up a whole new range of possibilities.

Pattern

Medium circle loom (color A)
Wrap yarn 1 time around all 24 pegs. Cut yarn, leaving an extra long tail, and tie off at center back of flower.

Center (color A)
Using long tail, secure bloom with a fully sewn center. Leave bloom on the loom and weave in ends.

Weaving (color B)
Weave 4 petals (8 strands of yarn) together to make a large woven petal, as follows:

Step 1
Thread a 12" (30cm) length of yarn onto a yarn needle. Weave the yarn over the first petal strand and then under the second strand. Continue weaving over and then under all 8 strands alternately to complete the first row of weaving. Push the weaving gently toward the center of the bloom as you work, using your fingers or the needle. At the end of the first row, pull the yarn through, leaving a tail of about 2" (5cm) at the beginning.

Step 2
Now weave in the opposite direction, weaving over and then under the petal strands. Continue weaving back and forth until the first petal is almost completely woven.

Step 3
Leaving the flower on the loom, weave the remaining petals in the same way. Beware that the first petal is the most fiddly to weave; it will get easier with the other petals.

Step 4
Carefully pop the bloom off the loom. Close the top of the petals by gently pulling the upper end of the weaving yarn. If you have used a contrasting color, as here, the flower will now have a small pop of color at the end of each petal. Weave in ends.

Chart key

    fully sewn center

o   loom peg

↰   weave yarn

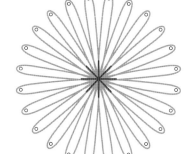
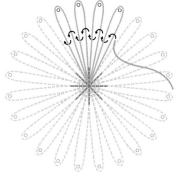
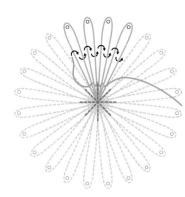

Shown at 105% actual size

VARIATIONS

- Use the same weaving color for all the petals (right), or alternate two colors (top and left).
- Weave over and under 2 strands at a time (instead of 1) with alternating colors (bottom).
- Weave 3 unwoven petals together (6 strands of yarn) to make a 12-petal flower (center).
- Weave the petals less densely (that is, with fewer horizontal rows of weaving), so that the long loops of the original petals remain visible.
- Experiment with other sizes and shapes of loom to create woven flowers.

Formal Flower Bed

The number of petals in your flower is not restricted to the number of pegs on the loom. Two petals are made from each loom peg in this pattern, creating a bloom that is reminiscent of hairpin lace crochet.

SKILL LEVEL:

DIAMETER: 4" (10cm)

Tools

Large circle loom

Crochet hook E/4 (3.5mm)

Yarn needle

Chart key

 star center

∘ loom peg

+ sc

dc

‒ whipstitch

Pattern

Large circle loom (color A)
Wrap yarn 2 times around all 24 pegs. Cut yarn, leaving an extra long tail, and tie off at center back of flower.

Center (color A)
Using long tail, secure bloom with a star center. Pop bloom off the loom and weave in ends.

Round 1 (color A)
Starting in any single petal loop: 1 sc in each of 48 petal loops. Join.

Round 2 (color B)
Starting in any sc: *1 dc in each of 3 sc, 2 dc in next sc; repeat from * 11 times. Join.

Joining motifs (color B of either motif)
Complete all motifs before joining. Place two motifs right sides together and join with whipstitch through both loops of each of 3 dc. Skip 12 dc around the circle before joining next motif. Weave in ends.

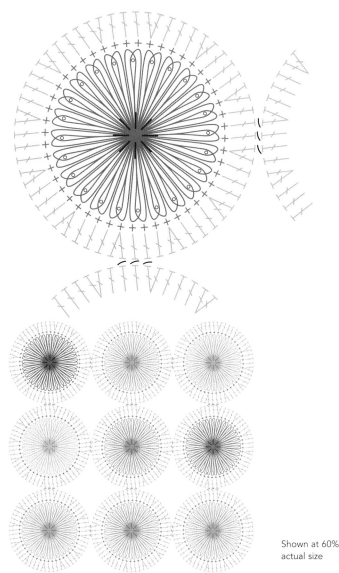

Shown at 60% actual size

Tales From My Garden

SKILL LEVEL: ✿ ✿ ✿
DIAMETER: 2¼" (5.5cm)

Tools

Medium circle loom

Small circle loom

Crochet hook E/4 (3.5mm)

Yarn needle

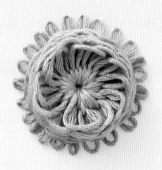

Chart key

 puffy star center

○ loom peg

⬯ ch

⬬ sl st

+ sc

⏜ together

This less common way of wrapping the yarn around the loom pegs creates a very different bloom with wide overlapping petals.

Pattern

Medium circle loom (color A throughout)

Wrap yarn 1 time around all 24 pegs in the usual way. Do not cut yarn.

Small circle loom

Now use a different wrapping technique for the small loom to make wide overlapping petals. Start by wrapping the yarn around two adjacent pegs at the top of the loom (pegs 1 and 2). Take the yarn across to the bottom of the loom and wrap it around the opposite two pegs in a figure-eight fashion. Take the yarn up to the top of the loom again and wrap it once again around peg 2 plus the adjacent peg 3. This petal will partially overlap the first petal, creating a layered effect. Work around the loom in this way as many times as possible to create a puffy bloom. In the sample shown, I managed to squeeze in 7 rounds. Cut yarn, leaving an extra long tail, and tie off at center back of flower.

Center

Using long tail, secure bloom with a puffy star center. Pop bloom off the loom and weave in ends.

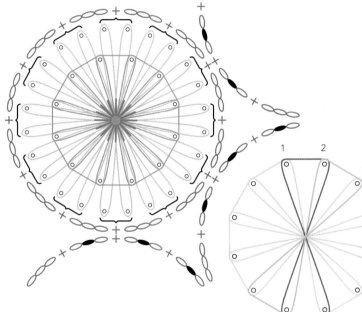

Round 1

Starting in any 2 medium petals and working through both loops together: *1 sc in 2 petals together, ch 3; repeat from * 11 times. Join.

Joining motifs

Complete first motif, then complete and join subsequent motifs on the go when working round 1, referring to charts for exact placement. Make a join by replacing the ch-3 between petals with: ch 1, sl st in ch-3 sp of adjoining motif, ch 1. Weave in ends.

Purple = 1st figure-eight wrap
Blue = 2nd figure-eight wrap
Continue in this way around loom

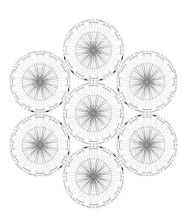

Shown at 90% actual size

Farmer's Market

I have a weak spot for big, uncomplicated blooms. This pattern was created as a memory of a lovely Saturday morning spent with friends at an eco-friendly farmer's market.

Pattern

Large circle loom (color A)
Wrap yarn 3 times around all 24 pegs. Cut yarn and tie off at center back of flower.

Center (color B)
Secure bloom with a puffy star center. Pop bloom off the loom and weave in ends.

Round 1 (color A)
Starting in any 4 petals and working through all 12 loops together: *1 sc in 4 petals together, ch 9; repeat from * 5 times. Join.

Joining motifs
Complete first motif, then complete and join subsequent motifs on the go when working round 1, referring to charts for exact placement. Make a join by replacing the ch-9 between petals with: ch 4, sl st in ch-9 sp of adjoining motif, ch 4. Weave in ends.

SKILL LEVEL: 🌸
DIAMETER: 3⅛" (8cm)

Tools

Large circle loom

Crochet hook E/4 (3.5mm)

Yarn needle

Chart key

 puffy star center

o   loom peg

⬭   ch

⬬   sl st

+   sc

︷   together

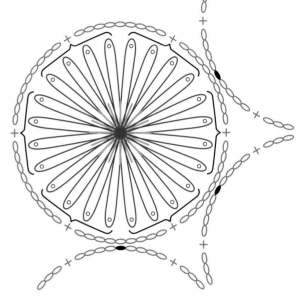

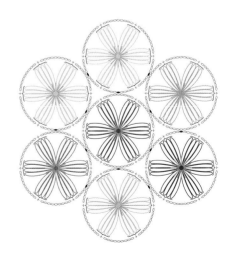

Shown at 70% actual size

SKILL LEVEL:

DIAMETER: 2¼" (5.5cm) excluding corner loops; 2½" (6.5cm) with loops

Tools

Medium circle loom

Crochet hook E/4 (3.5mm)

Yarn needle

Chart key

⁂	star center
o	loom peg
⬭	ch
⬮	sl st
+	sc
⏜	together

Go Green

There is something about the cute fluffiness of these flowers in a simple setting that makes this motif one of my personal favorites.

Pattern

Medium circle loom (color A)
Wrap yarn 2 times around all 24 pegs. Cut yarn and tie off at center back of flower.

Center (color B)
Secure bloom with a star center. Pop bloom off the loom and weave in ends.

Round 1 (color B)
Starting in any 2 petals and working through all 4 loops together: *1 sc in 2 petals together, ch 2, 1 sc in next 2 petals together, ch 2, [1 sc, ch 7, 1 sc] in next 2 petals together, ch 2; repeat from * 3 times. Join.

Joining motifs
Complete first motif, then complete and join subsequent motifs on the go when working round 1, referring to charts for exact placement. Make a join by replacing the corner ch-7 with: ch 3, sl st in ch-7 sp of adjoining motif, ch 3. Weave in ends.

VARIATION
Looking for a slightly different, more condensed look? You can join the motifs at the middle of each side by replacing 1 ch with a sl st into the ch-2 sp of the adjoining motif. You can also omit the corner chain loops altogether.

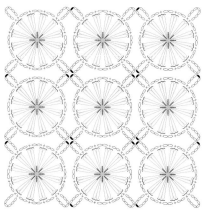

Shown at 90% actual size

Go Wild Flowers

This quintessential loom flower uses all three circle looms and lots of color. Go for it!

SKILL LEVEL: ❀
DIAMETER: 3" (7.5cm)

Tools

Large circle loom

Medium circle loom

Small circle loom

Yarn needle

Chart key

  flower bud
center

o   loom peg

✳   knot

Pattern

Large circle loom (color A)
Wrap yarn 3 times around all 24 pegs. Cut yarn and tie off at center back of flower.

Medium circle loom (color B)
Wrap yarn 1 time around all 24 pegs. Cut yarn and tie off at center back of flower.

Small circle loom (color C)
Wrap yarn 1 time around all 12 pegs. Cut yarn, leaving an extra long tail, and tie off at center back of flower.

Center (color C)
Using long tail, create a flower bud center with the small petals. (I strongly recommend that you work extra backstitches when doing so because of the number of loops.) Pop bloom off the loom and weave in ends.

Joining motifs (color A)
Complete all motifs before joining. Referring to charts for exact placement, turn motifs over to wrong side and use a 4" (10cm) length of yarn to join the lowest loops of the large

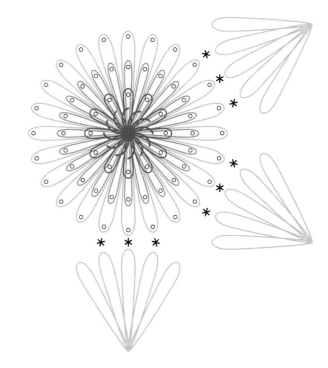

petals together with a double knot. Join three adjacent large petals, then skip 1 petal around the circle before joining the next motif. Make sure the remaining (untied) loops of the large petals mingle to create a lush effect. Take yarn tails to center back of bloom and weave in ends.

Shown at 80% actual size

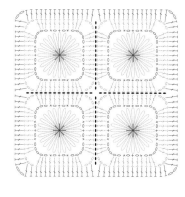

Cherry Blossom

Ah, these flowers remind me of the stunning cherry tree orchards of my youth. This easy-peasy pattern only requires one loom to create all this frivolous fluffiness.

SKILL LEVEL: ❀❀

WIDTH: 2¾" (7cm)

Tools

Medium circle loom

Crochet hook E/4 (3.5mm)

Yarn needle

Chart key

  fully sewn center

o loom peg

⬭ ch

⬮ sl st

+ sc

↑ dc

Pattern

Medium circle loom (color A)
Wrap yarn 5 times around all 24 pegs. Cut yarn and tie off at center back of flower.

Center (color B)
Secure bloom with a fully sewn center. Pop bloom off the loom and weave in ends.

Round 1 (color B)
Starting in any petal and working through lowest loop only (4 loops remain loose): *1 sc in petal, [ch 1, 1 sc in next petal] 2 times, ch 5, skip 3 petals; repeat from * 3 times. Join.

Round 2 (color B)
Starting in any corner ch-5 sp: *[3 dc, ch 3, 3 dc] in ch-5 sp, [1 dc in next sc, 1 dc in ch-1 sp] 2 times, 1 dc in next sc; repeat from * 3 times. Join.

Joining motifs (color B)
Complete all motifs before joining. Place two motifs right sides together and join by working sl st through back loops of each st along one side, from middle ch of one corner to the other. Without cutting yarn, join the next two motifs together in the same way. When the motifs are joined horizontally, repeat along the vertical sides. Weave in ends.

Border (color A)
Starting in any corner ch-3 sp: *[2 dc, ch 2, 2 dc] in ch-3 sp, work 1 dc in each of 11 dc along side of each motif, and 2 dc in each ch sp where motifs adjoin; repeat from * 3 times. Join. Weave in ends.

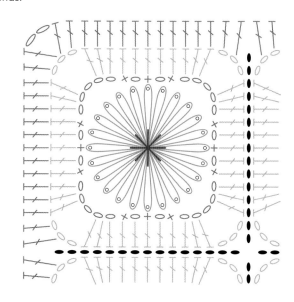

Shown at actual size

Stockholm Gardens

This dense yet sophisticated motif really stands apart from the average loom bloom. Make it in your favorite colors for a beautiful throw.

SKILL LEVEL:

WIDTH: 1¾" (4.5cm)

Tools

Small square loom

Crochet hook E/4 (3.5mm)

Yarn needle

Stitch markers

Chart key

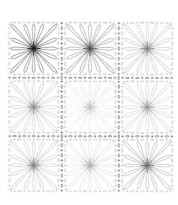 (chart key symbols)

✳   fully sewn center

o   loom peg

O   ch

+   sc

Pattern

Small square loom (color A)
Wrap yarn 2 times around all 16 pegs. Cut yarn, leaving an extra long tail, and tie off at center back of flower.

Center (color A)
Using long tail, secure bloom with a fully sewn center. Mark each corner petal (2 loops) with a stitch marker. Pop bloom off the loom and weave in ends.

Round 1 (color A)
Starting in any corner petal and working through both loops together: *[1 sc, ch 1, 1 sc] in corner petal, [ch 1, 1 sc in next petal] 3 times, ch 1; repeat from * 3 times. Join.

Joining motifs (color A or contrasting color)
Complete all motifs before joining. Place two motifs right sides together and join by working through both motifs together as follows: *1 sc in corner ch-1 sp, [ch 1, 1 sc in next ch-1 sp] 4 times, ch 1, 1 sc in corner ch-1 sp. Without cutting yarn, ch 1 and then repeat from * to join the next two motifs. When the motifs are joined horizontally, repeat along the vertical sides. Weave in ends.

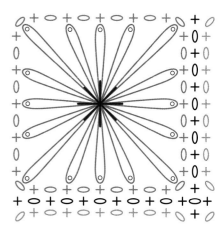

Shown at 90% actual size

Pretty Posy

The basic crochet frame really makes the flowers take the spotlight—simple loveliness.

SKILL LEVEL:

WIDTH: 2⅜" (6cm)

Tools

Medium circle loom

Crochet hook E/4 (3.5mm)

Yarn needle

Pattern

Medium circle loom (color A)
Wrap yarn 3 times around 12 pegs, skipping every other peg. Cut yarn and tie off at center back of flower.

Center (color B)
Secure bloom with a star center. Pop bloom off the loom and weave in ends.

Round 1 (color B)
Starting in any petal and working through lowest 2 loops only (1 loop remains loose): *[3-dc cluster, ch 3, 3-dc cluster] in petal (corner made), [ch 3, 1 sc in next petal] 2 times, ch 3; repeat from * 3 times. Join.

Joining motifs
Complete first motif, then complete and join subsequent motifs on the go when working round 1, referring to charts for exact placement. Make a join by replacing each ch-3 (at corners and along side) with: ch 1, sl st in ch-3 sp of adjoining motif, ch 1. Weave in ends.

Chart key

	star center
○	loom peg
⬭	ch
⬮	sl st
+	sc
⋔	3-dc cluster

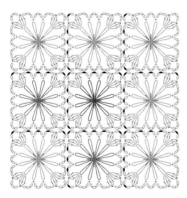

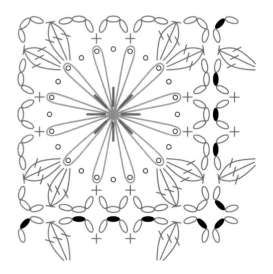

Shown at 90% actual size

Blooms of the Desert

SKILL LEVEL: 🌼
WIDTH: 1¼" (3cm)

Tools

Small circle loom

Yarn needle

Stitch markers

Chart key

✳	fully sewn center
○	loom peg
✳	knot
⏜	together

This is not your average loom bloom, and is another one of my personal favorites. The tactile puffiness combined with a strict geometrical pattern makes it a real eye-catcher.

Pattern

Small circle loom (color A throughout)

Wrap yarn 5 times around all 12 pegs. Cut yarn, leaving an extra long tail, and tie off at center back of flower.

Center

Using long tail, secure bloom with a fully sewn center. Pop bloom off the loom and weave in ends.

Step 1

Using a stitch marker, secure the first 3 petals (15 loops) together so that they form a large puffy petal. Repeat to make 4 puffy petals in total.

Step 2

Turn flower over to wrong side. Thread a 4" (10cm) length of yarn through all 15 loops of each puffy petal and tie a double knot to secure. Take yarn tails to center back of bloom and weave in ends.

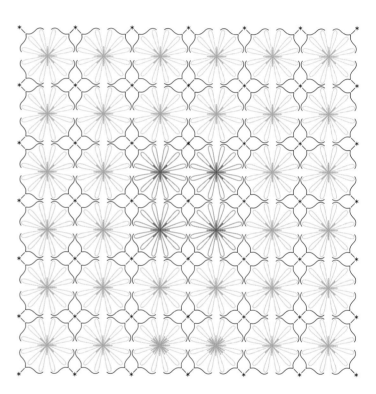

Joining motifs

Complete first motif, then complete and join subsequent motifs on the go when working step 2, referring to charts for exact placement. Make a join by tying the yarn through a puffy petal of the adjoining motif at the same time as the working motif. Weave in ends.

Shown at 70% actual size

Happy Harvest

Little square flowers captured in a simple crochet frame create an enchanting pattern that is great for blankets. It would also look good in a monochrome color scheme.

Pattern

Small square loom (color A)
Wrap yarn 3 times around all 16 pegs. Cut yarn, leaving an extra long tail, and tie off at center back of flower.

Center (color A)
Using long tail, secure bloom with a fully sewn center. Mark each corner petal (3 loops) with a stitch marker. Pop bloom off the loom and weave in ends.

Round 1 (color B)
Starting in any corner petal and working through all 3 loops

together: *[1 sc, ch 3, 1 sc] in corner petal, [ch 1, 1 sc in next petal] 3 times, ch 1; repeat from * 3 times. Join.

Round 2 (color B)
Starting in any corner ch-3 sp: *[2 dc, ch 3, 2 dc] in ch-3 sp, [2 dc in next ch-1 sp] 4 times; repeat from * 3 times. Join.

Joining motifs
Complete first motif, then complete and join subsequent motifs on the go when working round 2, referring to charts for

exact placement. Make a join at corners by replacing the corner ch-3 with: ch 1, sl st in ch-3 sp of adjoining motif, ch 1. Join the sides between every group of 2 dc by working a sl st between corresponding groups of 2 dc on adjoining motif. This creates a slightly ribbed join. Weave in ends.

SKILL LEVEL:

WIDTH: 2½" (6.5cm)

Tools

Small square loom

Crochet hook E/4 (3.5mm)

Yarn needle

Stitch markers

Chart key

✳	fully sewn center
∘	loom peg
⬯	ch
⬬	sl st
+	sc
†	dc

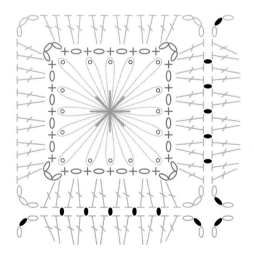

Shown at 90% actual size

Fall Wedding Bouquet

These simple blooms set in a delicate crochet framework create a beautiful motif with classic charm.

SKILL LEVEL: ✿ ✿ ✿

WIDTH: 4¼" (11cm)

Tools

Small circle loom

Crochet hook E/4 (3.5mm)

Yarn needle

Chart key

✳	puffy fully sewn center
∘	loom peg
⊘	ch
⬮	sl st
+	sc
†	dc
‡	joined dc

Pattern

Small circle loom (color A)
Wrap yarn 5 times around all 12 pegs. Cut yarn, leaving an extra long tail, and tie off at center back of flower.

Center (color A)
Using long tail, secure bloom with a puffy fully sewn center. Pop bloom off the loom and weave in ends.

Round 1 (color B)
Starting in any petal and working through all 5 loops together: *1 sc in petal, ch 2, 1 sc in next petal, ch 5; repeat from * 5 times. Join.

Round 2 (color B)
Starting in any ch-2 sp: *1 sc in ch-2 sp, 7 dc in ch-5 sp; repeat from * 5 times. Join.

Round 3 (color C)
Starting in any sc: * 1 dc in sc, ch 4, skip 3 dc, 1 sc in next dc, ch 4, skip 3 dc, 1 dc in next sc, ch 7, skip 3 dc, 1 sc in next dc, ch 4, skip 3 dc, 1 dc in next sc, ch 4, skip 3 dc, 1 sc in next dc, ch 7; repeat from * once. Join.

Round 4 (color C)
Starting in any corner ch-7 sp: *[5 dc, ch 3, 5 dc] in ch-7 sp, [5 dc in next ch-4 sp] 2 times; repeat from * 3 times. Join.

Joining motifs
Complete first motif, then complete and join subsequent motifs on the go when working round 4, referring to charts for exact placement. Make a join at corners by replacing the corner ch-3 with: ch 1, sl st in ch-3 sp of adjoining motif, ch 1. On the sides, work each dc as far as the last yo, then insert hook through back loop of dc on adjoining motif, yo and pull through all loops on hook. Weave in ends.

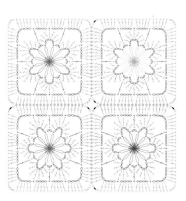

Shown at 70% actual size

VARIATION
The top row of motifs are oriented with one point of the inner crochet hexagon upward, while those in the bottom row have two points upward. You can vary the orientation in any way you like.

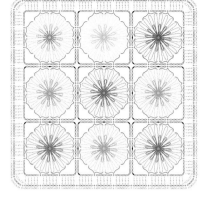

Florist's Dream

I love this one so much! Due to its laciness, the fabric has a marvelous drape. Believe me, you will just want to cuddle this one.

SKILL LEVEL: ❀ ❀

WIDTH: 3" (7.5cm)

Tools

Large circle loom

Small circle loom

Crochet hook E/4 (3.5mm)

Yarn needle

Chart key

☀ puffy star center

∘ loom peg

⬭ ch

⬬ sl st

+ sc

┬ dc

⏜ together

Pattern

Large circle loom (color A)
Wrap yarn 3 times around all 24 pegs. Cut yarn and tie off at center back of flower.

Small circle loom (color B)
Wrap yarn 3 times around all 12 pegs. Cut yarn, leaving an extra long tail, and tie off at center back of flower.

Center (color B)
Using long tail, secure bloom with a puffy star center. Pop bloom off the loom and weave in ends.

Round 1 (color A)
Starting in any 3 large petals and working through all 9 loops together: *1 sc in 3 petals together, ch 5, 1 sc in next 3 petals together, ch 9; repeat from * 3 times. Join.

Joining motifs
Complete first motif, then complete and join subsequent motifs on the go when working round 1, referring to charts for exact placement. Make a join by replacing the middle ch of each ch-9 and ch-5 (at corners and along sides) with: sl st in corresponding ch sp of adjoining motif. Weave in ends.

Border
Round 1 (color A)
Starting in any corner ch-9 sp: *[5 dc, ch 2, 5 dc] in ch-9 sp; work 5 dc in each ch-5 sp along sides of each motif, and 5 dc in each ch sp where motifs adjoin; repeat from * 3 times. Join.

Round 2 (color C)
Starting in any corner ch-2 sp: *[1 sc, ch 3, 1 sc] in ch-2 sp, ch 5, [1 sc in space between next two groups of 5 dc, ch 5] to next corner ch-2 sp; repeat from * 3 times. Join.

Round 3 (color A)
Starting in last sc before any corner ch-3 sp: *1 sc in sc, ch 3, [1 sc in next sc, ch 5] to last sc before next corner ch-3 sp; repeat from * 3 times. Join. Weave in ends.

Shown at 70% actual size

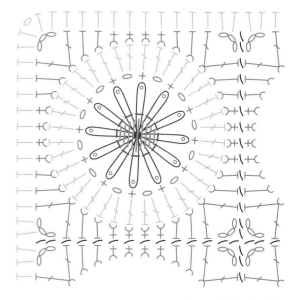

Doting on Dots

Striking dots are never boring, especially when captured in cheerful colors. You could also omit the squares to create lovely little circles, perfect for garlands and more.

Tools

Small circle loom

Crochet hook E/4 (3.5mm)

Yarn needle

Sharp embroidery needle

Stitch markers

Chart key

 oversewn backstitch center

o   loom peg

⟲   ch

+   sc

T   hdc

𝖳   dc

⌢   through back loop only

⁃   whipstitch

Pattern

Small circle loom (color A)
Wrap yarn 5 times around all 12 pegs. Cut yarn, leaving an extra long tail, and tie off at center back of flower.

Center (colors A and B)
Using long tail of color A, secure bloom with a backstitch center. With color B and sharp needle, fill the backstitch center with parallel lines of straight stitches, oversewing from side to side across the whole center. Mark each petal (5 loops) with a stitch marker. Pop bloom off the loom and weave in ends.

Round 1 (color C)
Starting in any petal and working through lowest loop only (4 loops remain loose): *1 sc in petal, ch 1; repeat from * 11 times. Join.

Round 2 (color C)
Starting in any sc: *1 dc in sc, 2 dc in ch-1 sp; repeat from * 11 times. Join.

Round 3 (color D)
Starting in any dc and working through back loops only: *1 sc in each of 4 dc, 1 hdc in each of next 2 dc, [1 dc, ch 3, 1 dc] in next dc, 1 hdc in each of next 2 dc; repeat from * 3 times. Join.

Joining motifs (color D)
Complete all motifs before joining. Place two motifs right sides together and join with whipstitch through back loops of each st along one side, from middle ch of one corner to the other. Without cutting yarn, join the next two motifs together in the same way. When the motifs are joined horizontally, repeat along the vertical sides. Weave in ends.

Border (color D)
Starting in any corner ch-3 sp: *[2 hdc, ch 1, 2 hdc] in ch-3 sp, work 1 hdc in each of 10 sts along side of each motif, and 2 hdc in each ch sp where motifs adjoin; repeat from * 3 times. Join. Weave in ends.

Shown at 80% actual size

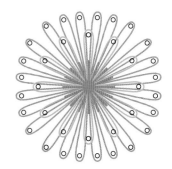

Bucolic Blossom

With two phases of a blossom captured in one pattern, these motifs would be lovely for a spring blanket sprinkled with blossoms.

SKILL LEVEL: 🌸🌸🌸
WIDTH: 4⅛" (10.5cm)

Tools

Medium circle loom

Small circle loom

Crochet hook E/4 (3.5mm)

Yarn needle

Chart key

 flower bud center

 puffy fully sewn center

∘   loom peg

⬯   ch

⬮   sl st

+   sc

⊤   dc

Pattern

Medium circle loom (color A)
Wrap yarn 5 times around all 24 pegs. Cut yarn and tie off at center back of flower.

Small circle loom (color B)
Wrap yarn 1 time around all 12 pegs. Cut yarn, leaving an extra long tail, and tie off at center back of flower.

Center (color B)
To make a flower bud (top left motif), create a flower bud center using the long tail and small petals. To make an open blossom (bottom right motif), secure bloom with a puffy fully sewn center. Pop bloom off the loom and weave in ends.

Both flower motifs (color B)
Round 1: Starting in any medium petal and working through lowest loop only (4 loops remain loose): *1 sc in each of 6 petals, ch 5 (corner made); repeat from * 3 times. Join.
Round 2: Starting in any corner ch sp: *[2 dc, ch 2, 2 dc] in ch sp, 1 dc in each st along side; repeat from * 3 times. Join.
Round 3: As round 2.

Crochet motif (color A)
Make a magic ring, or ch 4 and join with sl st to form a ring.
Round 1: [2 dc, ch 2] 4 times into ring. Join. Each ch-2 forms a corner ch sp; the dc sts form the sides of the square.
Rounds 2–4: As round 2 of flower motif.

All motifs (color B)
Final round: Starting in any corner ch-2 sp: *[1 sc, ch 5, 1 sc] in ch-2 sp, [ch 5, skip 2 dc, 1 sc in next dc] 4 times, ch 5; repeat from * 3 times. Join.

Joining motifs
Complete first motif, then complete and join subsequent motifs on the go when working final round, referring to charts for exact placement. Make a join by replacing each ch-5 (at corners and along sides) with: ch 2, sl st in ch-5 sp of adjoining motif, ch 2. Weave in ends.

Shown at 70% actual size

Renaissance Garden

SKILL LEVEL: ❀❀
WIDTH: 2¼" (5.5cm)

This geometric motif is made by creating two petals from each loom peg. The pattern would make a classy and travel-friendly checkerboard.

Tools
. . . .
Small circle loom

Crochet hook E/4 (3.5mm)

Yarn needle

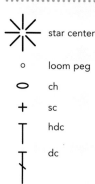

Chart key
. . . .

⁂ star center

o loom peg

⊙ ch

+ sc

T hdc

⊤ dc

Pattern

Small circle loom (color A)
Wrap yarn 2 times around all 12 pegs. Cut yarn, leaving an extra long tail, and tie off at center back of flower.

Center (color A)
Using long tail, secure bloom with a star center. Pop bloom off the loom and weave in ends.

Round 1 (color B)
Starting in any single petal loop: 1 sc in each of 24 petal loops. Join.

Round 2 (color B)
Starting in any sc: *1 sc in sc, 1 hdc in next sc, 1 dc in next sc, [1 dc, ch 3, 1 dc] in next sc, 1 dc in next sc, 1 hdc in next sc; repeat from * 3 times. Join.

Joining motifs (color B)
Complete all motifs before joining. Place two motifs right sides together and join by working sc though back loops of each st along one side, from middle ch of one corner to the other. Without cutting yarn, join the next two motifs in the same way. When the motifs are joined horizontally, repeat along the vertical sides. Weave in ends.

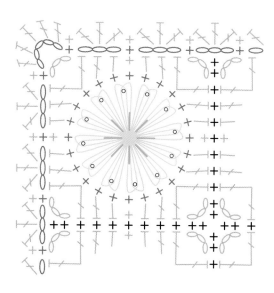

Border (color A or B)
Round 1
Starting in any corner ch-3 sp: *[1 sc, ch 5, 1 sc] in ch-3 sp; along side of each motif work ch 3, skip 3 sts, 1 sc in sc, ch 3, skip 3 sts; where two motifs adjoin work 1 sc in first ch sp, ch 3, 1 sc in next ch sp; repeat from * 3 times. Join.

Round 2
Starting in any corner ch-5 sp: *5 dc in ch-5 sp, 1 sc in next sc, [3 dc in ch-3 sp, 1 sc in next sc] to next corner ch-5 sp; repeat from * 3 times. Join. Weave in ends.

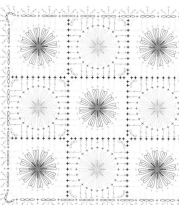

Shown at 90% actual size

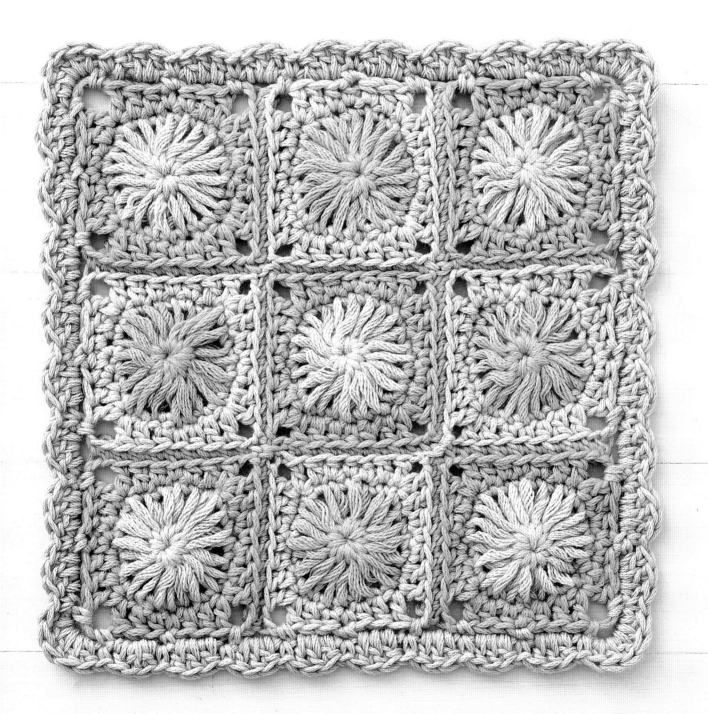

Flower Fair

This pattern would make a beautiful throw. You could use a thicker yarn and wrap the yarn fewer times around the loom pegs to speed up the process.

SKILL LEVEL:

WIDTH: 4" (10cm)

Tools

Large square loom

Crochet hook E/4 (3.5mm)

Yarn needle

Stitch markers

Chart key

✳ fully sewn center

○ loom peg

⬭ ch

⬬ sl st

+ sc

† dc

Pattern

Large square loom (color A)
Wrap yarn 3 times around all 32 pegs. Cut yarn, leaving an extra long tail, and tie off at center back of flower.

Center (color A)
Using long tail, secure bloom with a fully sewn center. Mark each petal (3 loops) with a stitch marker—or at least mark each corner petal. Pop bloom off the loom and weave in ends.

Round 1 (color B)
Starting in any corner petal and working through all 3 loops together: *[1 sc, ch 2, 1 sc] in corner petal, [ch 1, 1 sc in next petal] 7 times, ch 1; repeat from * 3 times. Join.

Round 2 (color B)
Starting in any corner ch-2 sp: *[1 dc, ch 3, 1 dc] in ch-2 sp, ch 1, [1 sc in next ch-1 sp, ch 3] 7 times, 1 sc in next ch-1 sp, ch 1; repeat from * 3 times. Join.

Joining motifs
Complete first motif, then complete and join subsequent motifs on the go when working round 2, referring to charts for exact placement. Make a join by replacing each ch-3 (at corners and along sides) with: ch 1, sl st in ch-3 sp of adjoining motif, ch 1. Weave in ends.

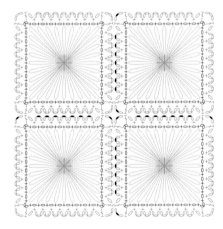

Shown at 80% actual size

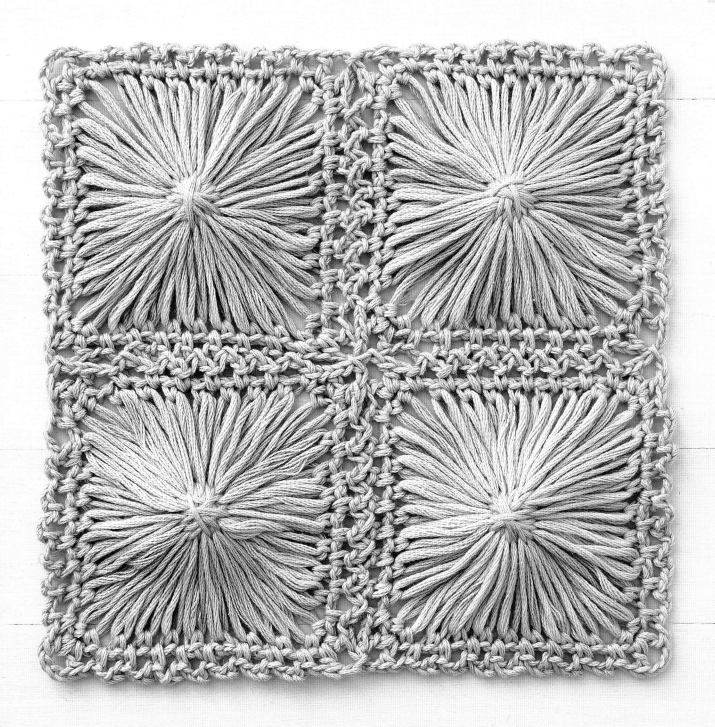

The Conservatory

What I like about this pattern is the combination of circles and squares. They blend nicely together to produce a soft, lacy motif.

SKILL LEVEL: ✿✿
WIDTH: 3½" (9cm)

Tools

Large circle loom

Small circle loom

Crochet hook E/4 (3.5mm)

Yarn needle

Chart key

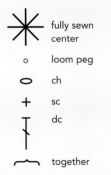

✳   fully sewn center

o   loom peg

⬭   ch

+   sc

┬   dc

⌣   together

Pattern

Large circle loom (color A)
Wrap yarn 1 time around all 24 pegs. Cut yarn and tie off at center back of flower.

Small circle loom (color B)
Wrap yarn 3 times around all 12 pegs. Cut yarn, leaving an extra long tail, and tie off at center back of flower.

Center (color B)
Using long tail, secure bloom with a fully sewn center. Pop bloom off the loom and weave in ends.

Round 1 (color C)
Starting in any 2 large petals and working through both loops together: *[1 sc in 2 petals together] 3 times, ch 7; repeat from * 3 times. Join.

Round 2 (color C)
Starting in any ch-7 sp: *[5 dc, ch 2, 5 dc] in ch-7 sp, 1 dc in each of next 3 sc; repeat from * 3 times. Join.

Round 3 (color D)
Starting in any ch-2 sp: *3 sc in ch-2 sp, 1 sc in each of next 13 dc; repeat from * 3 times. Join.

Joining motifs
Complete all motifs before joining. Place two motifs right sides together and join by working sc though both loops of each st along one side, from middle sc of one corner to the other. Without cutting yarn, join the next two motifs in the same way. When the motifs are joined horizontally, repeat along the vertical sides. Weave in ends.

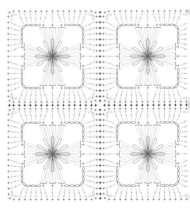

Shown at 90% actual size

What You Sow

This is such a versatile pattern—I'm thinking blankets, tablecloths…

SKILL LEVEL: ✿

WIDTH: 4¼" (11cm)

Tools

Large circle loom

Crochet hook E/4 (3.5mm)

Yarn needle

Chart key

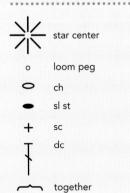

☀	star center
o	loom peg
⬭	ch
⬬	sl st
+	sc
┬	dc
⌣	together

Pattern

Large circle loom (color A)

Wrap yarn 1 time around all 24 pegs. Cut yarn, leaving an extra long tail, and tie off at center back of flower.

Center (color A)

Using long tail, secure bloom with a star center. Pop bloom off the loom and weave in ends.

Round 1 (color B)

Starting in any 2 petals and working through both loops together: *1 sc in 2 petals together, ch 5, 1 sc in next 2 petals together, ch 5, [1 dc, ch 5, 1 dc] in next 2 petals together, ch 5; repeat from * 3 times. Join.

Round 2 (color B)

Starting in any corner ch-5 sp between 2 dc: * [2 dc, ch 3, 2 dc] in ch-5 sp, ch 3, [1 sc in next ch-5 sp, ch 5] 2 times, 1 sc in next ch-5 sp, ch 3; repeat from * 3 times. Join.

Joining motifs

Complete first motif, then complete and join subsequent motifs on the go when working round 2, referring to charts for exact placement. Make a join by replacing the middle ch of each ch-3 and ch-5 (at corners and along sides) with: sl st in corresponding ch sp of adjoining motif. Weave in ends.

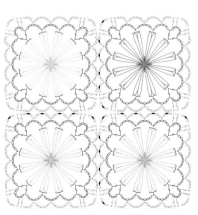

Shown at 70% actual size

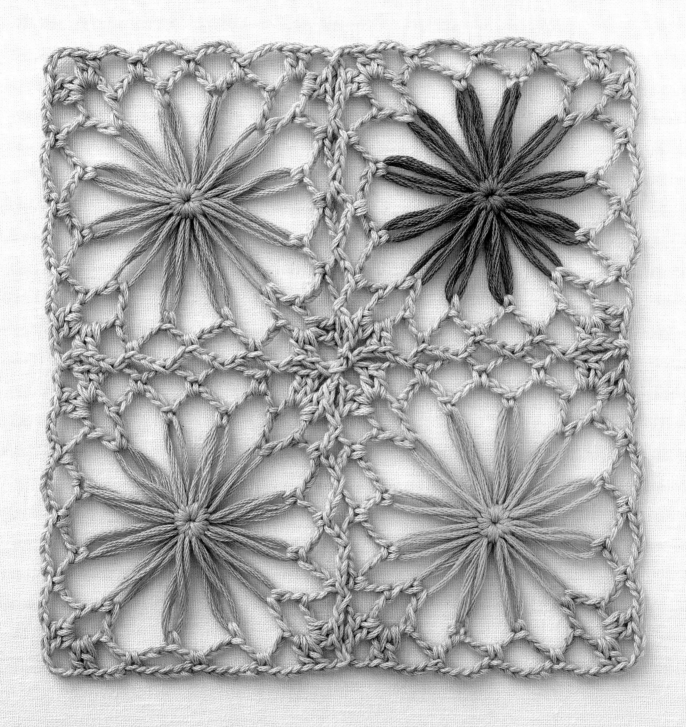

Spring Bouquet

Be still my beating heart! I adore these simple blooms set in hexagons. The puffy flower bud centers add a quaint touch.

SKILL LEVEL: ✿

DIAMETER: 3½" (9cm)

Tools

Medium circle loom

Small circle loom

Crochet hook E/4 (3.5mm)

Yarn needle

Chart key

 flower bud center

○   loom peg

⬭   ch

⬬   sl st

+   sc

𝄐   dc

Pattern

Medium circle loom (color A)
Wrap yarn 3 times around 12 pegs, skipping every other peg. Cut yarn and tie off at center back of flower.

Small circle loom (color B)
Wrap yarn 3 times around all 12 pegs. Cut yarn, leaving an extra long tail, and tie off at center back of flower.

Center (color B)
Using long tail, create a flower bud center with the small petals. Pop bloom off the loom and weave in ends.

Round 1 (color C)
Starting in any medium petal and working through all 3 loops together: *1 sc in petal, ch 2, 1 sc in next petal, ch 4; repeat from * 5 times. Join.

Round 2 (color C)
Starting in any ch-2 sp: *2 dc in ch-2 sp, 1 dc in next sc, [2 dc, ch 2, 2 dc] in ch-4 sp, 1 dc in next sc; repeat from * 5 times. Join.

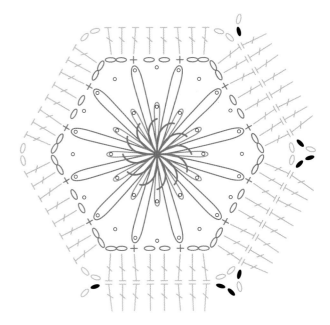

Joining motifs
Complete first motif, then complete and join subsequent motifs on the go when working round 2, referring to charts for exact placement. Make a join at the ch-2 corners by replacing 1 ch (the ch nearest the 8-dc side being joined) with a sl st into the ch-2 sp of the adjoining motif, or replace 2 ch with a sl st into each ch-2 sp when there are two adjoining motifs. Weave in ends.

Shown at 70% actual size

Summer of Love

I loved creating this motif. The puffy, colorful flowers are very easy to make and never cease to make me smile. The crocheted hexagon border creates an elegant finish.

SKILL LEVEL: ❀ ❀
DIAMETER: 2½" (6.5cm)

Tools

Small circle loom

Crochet hook E/4 (3.5mm)

Yarn needle

Chart key

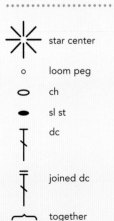

✳   star center

o   loom peg

◠   ch

⬬   sl st

┃   dc

╪   joined dc

⌣   together

Pattern

Small circle loom (color A)

Wrap yarn 5 times around all 12 pegs. Cut yarn and tie off at center back of flower.

Center (color B)

Secure bloom with a star center. Pop bloom off the loom and weave in ends.

Round 1 (color C)

Starting in any 2 petals and working through all 10 loops together: *Sl st in 2 petals together, ch 3; repeat from * 5 times. Join.

Round 2 (color C)

Starting in any sl st: *1 dc in sl st, [2 dc, ch 2, 2 dc] in ch-3 sp; repeat from * 5 times. Join.

Joining motifs

Complete first motif, then complete and join subsequent motifs on the go when working round 2, referring to charts for exact placement. Make a join at the ch-2 corners by replacing 1 ch (the ch nearest the 5-dc side being joined) with a sl st into the ch-2 sp of the adjoining motif, or replace 2 ch with a sl st into each ch-2 sp when there are two adjoining motifs. On the sides, work each dc as far as the last yo, then insert hook through back loop of dc on adjoining motif, yo and pull through all loops on hook. Weave in ends.

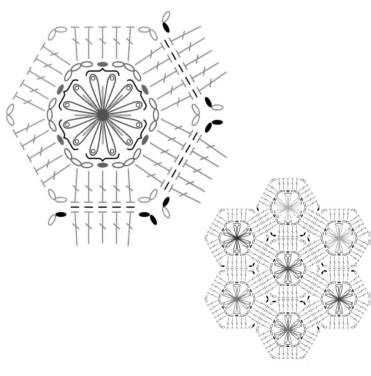

Shown at 90% actual size

TIP
These hexagons are joined at the corners and in each stitch along the sides, which creates a slightly ribbed effect. This is a very secure way of joining motifs, ideal for items such as blankets.

Garden House Grace

This is an addictive pattern to make, and it works up fairly quickly. I am planning to make a curtain with this motif using a fingering yarn.

SKILL LEVEL: ❀ ❀ ❀
DIAMETER: 5½" (14cm)

Tools

Medium circle loom

Crochet hook E/4 (3.5mm)

Yarn needle

Chart key

✳	fully sewn center
o	loom peg
⬮	ch
⬤	sl st
+	sc
T	hdc
ᵀ	dc
ǂ	tr

Pattern

Medium circle loom (color A throughout)

Wrap yarn 3 times around 12 pegs, skipping every other peg. Cut yarn, leaving an extra long tail, and tie off at center back of flower.

Center

Using long tail, secure bloom with a fully sewn center. Pop bloom off the loom and weave in ends.

Round 1

Starting in any petal and working through all 3 loops together: *1 sc in each of 2 petals, ch 6; repeat from * 5 times. Join.

Round 2

Starting in any ch-6 sp: *[1 sc, 1 hdc, 2 dc, 1 tr, 2 dc, 1 hdc, 1 sc] in ch-6 sp (shell made), skip 2 sc; repeat from * 5 times. Join.

Round 3

Starting in space between any two shells: *1 sc in space between shells, ch 3, 1 dc in first dc of shell, ch 5, 1 dc in tr, ch 5, 1 dc in last dc of shell, ch 3; repeat from * 5 times. Join.

Round 4

Starting in first ch-3 sp of two consecutive ch-3 sps: *1 sc in ch-3 sp, ch 3, 1 sc in next ch-3 sp, ch 5, 1 dc in ch-5 sp, ch 5, 1 dc in next ch-5 sp, ch 5; repeat from * 5 times. Join.

Joining motifs

Complete first motif, then complete and join subsequent motifs on the go when working round 4, referring to charts for exact placement. Make a join by replacing the middle ch-5 of three consecutive ch-5 with ch 2, sl st in ch-5 sp of adjoining motif, ch 2. Weave in ends.

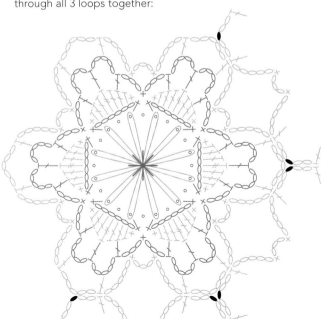

Shown at 50% actual size

Organic Flowers

After creating a couple of hexagon designs with solid crochet borders, I decided to design a lacier version. I like the result—simple and quick.

Tools

Small circle loom

Crochet hook E/4 (3.5mm)

Yarn needle

Chart key

⁎   fully sewn center

o   loom peg

⬭   ch

⬬   sl st

+   sc

⬙   2-dc cluster

⏜   together

Pattern

Small circle loom (color A)
Wrap yarn 2 times around all 12 pegs. Cut yarn, leaving an extra long tail, and tie off at center back of flower.

Center (color A)
Using long tail, secure bloom with a fully sewn center. Pop bloom off the loom and weave in ends.

Round 1 (color B)
Starting in any 2 petals and working through all 4 loops together: *1 sc in 2 petals together, ch 6; repeat from * 5 times. Join.

Round 2 (color B)
Starting in any sc: *[2-dc cluster, ch 5, 2-dc cluster] in sc, ch 3; repeat from * 5 times. Join.

Joining motifs
Complete first motif, then complete and join subsequent motifs on the go when working round 2, referring to charts for exact placement. Make a join by replacing the corner ch-5 with: ch 2, sl st in ch-5 sp of adjoining motif, ch 2. Weave in ends.

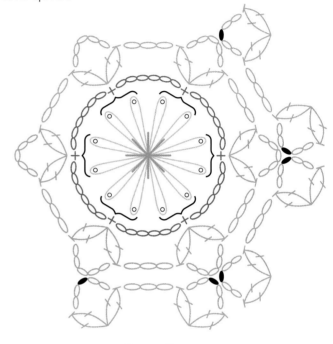

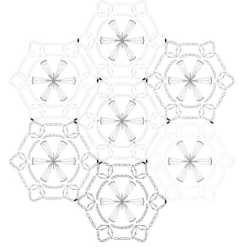

Shown at 90% actual size

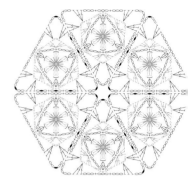

Butterfly's Bliss

Not only butterflies fall for this motif. Want more triangles? In the tutorial on page 22, I show you how to make a triangle directly on the loom.

SKILL LEVEL:

SIZE: 7½" (19cm) diameter; each edge 3¾" (9.5cm)

Tools

Small circle loom

Crochet hook E/4 (3.5mm)

Yarn needle

Chart key

	puffy star center
∘	loom peg
⬯	ch
⬬	sl st
+	sc
┬	dc
	3-dc cluster
⏜	together

Pattern

Small circle loom (color A)
Wrap yarn 4 times around all 12 pegs. Cut yarn, leaving an extra long tail, and tie off at center back of flower.

Center (color A)
Using long tail, secure bloom with a puffy star center. Pop bloom off the loom and weave in ends.

Round 1 (color B)
Starting in any 2 petals and working through all 8 loops together: *1 sc in 2 petals together, ch 4, 3-dc cluster in next 2 petals together, ch 4; repeat from * 2 times. Join.

Round 2 (color B)
Starting in any cluster: *1 sc in cluster, ch 3, [3 dc, ch 3, 3 dc] in sc, ch 3; repeat from * 2 times. Join.

Round 3 (color C)
Starting in any ch-3 sp between two groups of 3 dc: *[3 dc, ch 5, 3 dc] in ch-3 sp, [ch 3, 1 sc in next ch-3 sp] 2 times, ch 3; repeat from * 2 times. Join.

Joining motifs
Complete first motif, then complete and join subsequent motifs on the go when working round 3, referring to charts for exact placement. Make a join by replacing the middle ch of each ch-5 and ch-3 (at corners and along sides) with: sl st in corresponding ch sp of adjoining motif. Weave in ends.

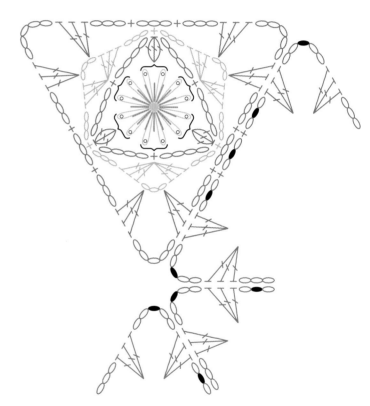

Shown at 90% actual size

TIP
You don't have to restrict yourself to joining just six triangles. You can treat these like large hexagons or join them in continuous rows of triangles.

My Little Flower Patch

You can create lovely effects by using different loom sizes in one round. This versatile motif entails wrapping the yarn around three looms at the same time. It would also be wonderful for creating snowflakes or stars.

SKILL LEVEL: ✿✿

DIAMETER: 3" (7.5cm)

Tools

Large circle loom

Medium circle loom

Small circle loom

Yarn needle

Chart key

✳ fully sewn center

○ loom peg

✳ knot

Pattern

All three looms (color A)

For this pattern you wrap the yarn around two opposite pegs on the same size loom (like you normally would), but then continue with two opposite pegs on a different size loom. Alternate loom sizes in this order: large, medium, small, medium. Continue in this order until you have completed the first round. Make three rounds like this in total. Cut yarn and tie off at center back of flower.

Center (color B)

Secure bloom with a fully sewn center. Pop bloom off the loom and weave in ends.

Joining motifs

Complete all motifs before joining. Referring to charts for exact placement, turn motifs over to wrong side and use a 4" (10cm) length of yarn to join the large petals together with a double knot. Take yarn tails to center back of bloom and weave in ends.

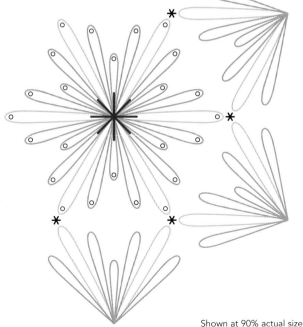

Shown at 90% actual size

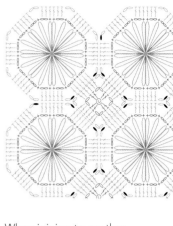

Regent's Park

Okay, so this isn't actually a hexagon, but octagons are such versatile shapes that I definitely wanted to include one in this book. You can vary the pattern by omitting the crochet squares.

SKILL LEVEL:

SIZE: octagon 4" (10cm) diameter; square 1½" (4cm) wide

Tools

Large circle loom

Crochet hook E/4 (3.5mm)

Yarn needle

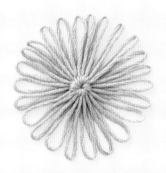

Chart key

✳ star center

o loom peg

C magic ring

o ch

— sl st

+ sc

⊺ dc

Pattern

Large circle loom (color A)
Wrap yarn 1 time around all 24 pegs. Cut yarn, leaving an extra long tail, and tie off at center back of flower.

Center (color A)
Using long tail, secure bloom with a star center. Pop bloom off the loom and weave in ends.

Round 1 (color A)
Starting in any petal: *1 sc in each of 2 petals, ch 2, 1 sc in next petal, ch 2; repeat from * 7 times. Join.

Round 2 (color A)
Starting in first sc of any group of 2 sc: *1 dc in each of 2 sc, 2 dc in ch-2 sp, ch 2, skip 1 sc, 2 dc in next ch-2 sp; repeat from * 7 times. Join.

Crochet squares (color B)
Make a magic ring, or ch 4 and join with sl st to form a ring.
Round 1: [2 dc, ch 2] 4 times into ring. Join.

Round 2: Starting in any ch-2 sp: *[2 dc, ch 2, 2 dc] in ch-2 sp, 1 dc in each of next 2 dc; repeat from * 3 times. Join.

Joining motifs
Complete the total number of crochet squares required for your project. Then complete and join the octagons on the go when working round 2, referring to charts for exact placement. Make a join by replacing 1 ch of each ch-2 corner with a sl st into ch-2 corner of adjoining motif.

When joining to another octagon (at outer corners), substitute the innermost ch of the ch-2 corner. When joining to a square, substitute the ch at each end of the 6-dc side. To make the joins almost invisible, work the sl st through the back loop of the adjacent ch in the adjoining motif, rather than into the ch-2 sp. This will stop the octagon color from bleeding through into the crochet squares. Weave in ends.

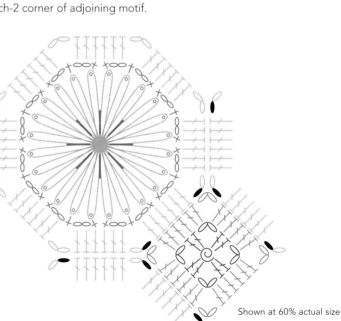

Shown at 60% actual size

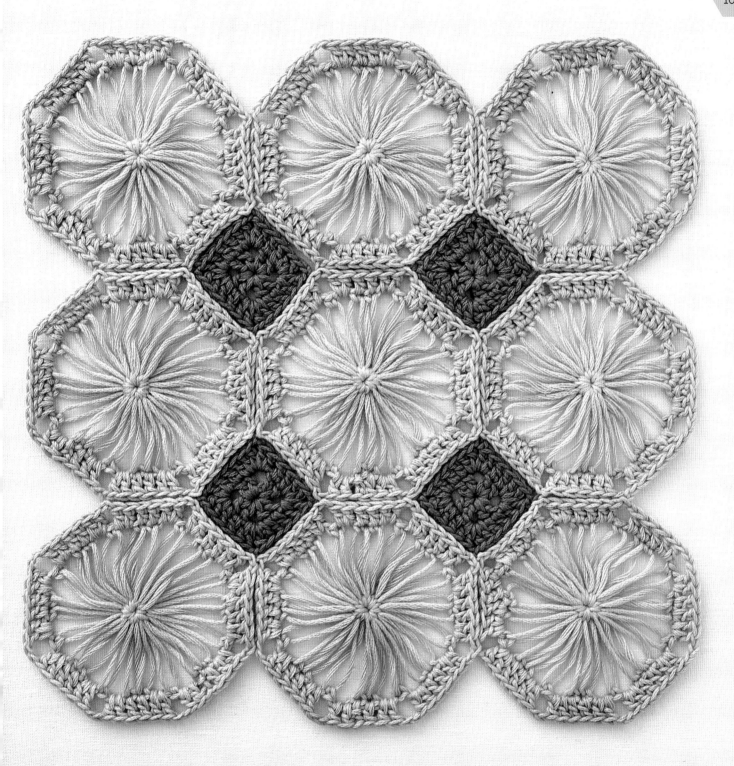

Projects

This chapter takes things a step further by showing you how to use loom flowers to create beautiful garments, accessories, and homewares. Why not try substituting different flower patterns for each project and experimenting with color to create items that are truly unique?

SKILL LEVEL: 🌸🌸🌸

SIZE: 5½" (14cm) square

Yarn

Sport-weight mercerized cotton yarn in 3 colors

A: pink 44yd (40m)

B: mint 33yd (30m)

C: white 137yd (125m)

Note: Choose wool yarn if you wish to put the potholder to practical use; wool resists burning and is a great insulator.

Tools

Small circle loom

Crochet hook C/2 or D/3 (3mm)

Yarn needle

Chart key

 fully sewn center

∘ loom peg

✳ knot

⊙ ch

⬤ sl st

+ sc

† dc

🜕 2-tr cluster

Vintage Potholder

Make this vintage-style potholder to add a certain "je ne sais quoi" to your kitchen decor. The crisp stitch definition of cotton yarn is perfect for decorative wall art, or use wool yarn for a more practical potholder.

Pattern

Front (color A)
Make and join four flowers according to the Blooms of the Desert pattern (page 76). Weave in ends.

Round 1 (color B)
Starting in space between any two flowers: *[2-tr cluster, ch 2, 2-tr cluster] in space between flowers, ch 2, [2-tr cluster, ch 2, 2-tr cluster, ch 2, 2-tr cluster] in corner petal, ch 2; repeat from * 3 times. Join.

Round 2 (color C)
Starting in middle cluster at any corner: *[2 dc, ch 3, 2 dc] in corner cluster, [3 dc in ch-2 sp, 1 dc in next cluster] 4 times, 3 dc in ch-2 sp; repeat from * 3 times. Join.

Round 3 (color C)
Starting in any corner ch-3 sp: *[2 dc, ch 3, 2 dc] in ch-3 sp, 1 dc in each dc along side; repeat from * 3 times. Join.

Round 4 (color C)
As round 3.

Round 5 (color B)
Starting in any corner ch-3 sp: *[1 sc, ch 5, 1 sc] in ch-3 sp, [ch 1, skip 1 dc, 1 sc in next dc, ch 3, skip 3 dc, 1 sc in next dc] 5 times, ch 1, skip 1 dc; repeat from * 3 times. Join.

Round 6 (color B)
Starting in any corner ch-5 sp and skipping all sc: *7 dc in ch-5 sp, [1 sc in ch-1 sp, 5 dc in ch-3 sp] 5 times, 1 sc in ch-1 sp; repeat from * 3 times. Join.

Back (color C)

Row 1: Ch 32, 1 dc in 3rd ch from hook, 1 dc in each ch to end, turn.

Row 2: Ch 2 (counts as 1 dc), 1 dc in each st to end, turn. (31 dc)

Rows 3–15: As row 2. Fasten off.

Joining front and back (color C)

Place front and back wrong sides together, with the edges of the back level with the edges of round 4 (color C) of the front. Join with whipstitch around all four sides; the stitches should be snug, but not tight. Cut yarn and weave in ends.

Hanging loop (color B)

Working on back of potholder, slip stitch into a corner, ch 15, sl st into same corner, turn, ch 1, 25 sc into ch-15 sp. Fasten off and weave in ends. You can make a shorter or longer loop as preferred.

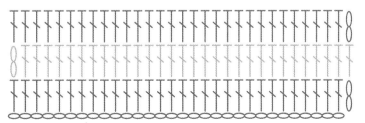

Back rows 1–3; repeat row 2 for 15 rows in total.

Hanging loop

SKILL LEVEL:
MOTIFS: 100 motifs,
each 2" (5cm) diameter
SCARF: 8 x 50" (20 x 125cm)

Yarn

Fingering-weight acrylic
yarn in 3 colors
A: off-white 110yd (100m)
B: dark gray 110yd (100m)
C: brown 110yd (100m)

Tools

Small circle loom
Crochet hook B/1
(2.25mm)
Yarn needle

Chart key

✳	fully sewn center
○	loom peg
⬯	ch
⬮	sl st
+	sc

Floating Flowers Scarf

This scarf works well with any outfit, from a smart business suit to a flowery dress. The simple rectangular shape makes it easy to adjust the length and width to suit your tastes. Simply add more motifs to make a pretty wrap or shawl.

Pattern

Small circle loom (color A)
Wrap yarn 1 time around all 12 pegs. Cut yarn and tie off at center back of flower.

Center (color B)
Secure bloom with a fully sewn center. Pop bloom off the loom and weave in ends.

Round 1 (color B or C)
Use color B for half the motifs and color C for the remainder. Starting in any petal: *1 sc in petal, ch 5; repeat from * 11 times. Join.

Joining motifs
The scarf consists of 25 rows of 4 motifs, arranged with alternating colors on round 1. Complete first motif, then complete and join subsequent motifs on the go when working round 1, referring to charts for exact placement. Make a join by replacing the ch-5 between petals with: ch 2, sl st in ch-5 sp of adjoining motif, ch 2. Weave in ends.

Continue adding rows of motifs, alternating colors as shown.

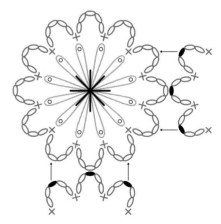

SKILL LEVEL: 🌼🌼
MOTIFS: 24 motifs,
each 3½" (9cm) square
BAG: 11 x 16" (28 x 40cm)
STRAP: 1 x 34" (2.5 x 86cm)

Yarn

Sport-weight mercerized
cotton yarn in 7 colors

A: yellow 46yd (42m)

B: chocolate 46yd (42m)

C: black 46yd (42m)

D: light pink 46yd (42m)

E: bright pink 46yd (42m)

F: mid-pink 96yd (87m)

G: white 296yd (270m)

Tools

Large square loom

Crochet hook C/2 or D/3
(3mm)

Yarn needle

Stitch markers

Chart key

✳   fully sewn
center

o   loom peg

⊙   ch

+   sc

┬   dc

Tote Bag

I looove tote bags, so I definitely wanted to include a
pattern for one in this book—and I am so happy with
the result. For me, this bag is the ultimate proof that
flower looming is an all-round craft, suitable for a wide
range of projects. This bag uses 24 flower motifs, but
you can make the bag any size you like.

Pattern

Large square loom (colors A–F)
Use each color to make the
flowers for 4 motifs. Wrap yarn
3 times around all 32 pegs.
Cut yarn, leaving an extra long
tail, and tie off at center back
of flower.

Center (colors A–F)
Using long tail, secure bloom with
a fully sewn center. This is a very
secure center, so it will make the
bag more durable. Mark each
petal (3 loops) with a stitch
marker—or at least mark each
corner petal. Pop bloom off the
loom and weave in ends.

Round 1 (color G)
Starting in any corner petal
and working through all 3 loops
together: *[1 sc, ch 2, 1 sc] in
corner petal, [ch 1, 1 sc] in each
of next 7 petals, ch 1; repeat from
* 3 times. Join.

Round 2 (color G)
Starting in any corner ch-2 sp:
*[2 dc, ch 3, 2 dc] in ch-2 sp,
1 dc in each sc and ch-1 sp
along side (17 dc); repeat from
* 3 times. Join.

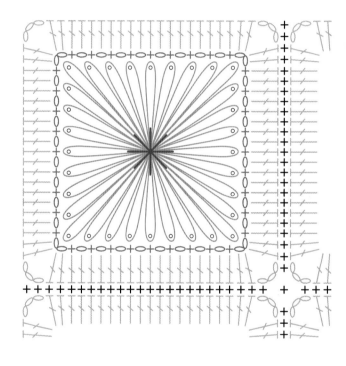

Joining motifs (color G)

Complete all motifs before joining. Arrange and join 12 motifs each for the front and back in any order you like; the placement of the colors does not have to match. Place two motifs right sides together and join by working through both motifs together as follows: 2 sc in corner ch-3 sp, 1 sc through both loops of each dc along side, 1 sc in corner ch-3 sp. Without cutting yarn, repeat to join the next two motifs. When the motifs are joined horizontally, repeat along the vertical sides. Weave in ends.

Border (color G)

The front and back each need a border before you can join the two pieces together. If you omit the border, the motifs at the sides will be "pulled" into the seam of the bag and so will not be completely visible. Starting in any corner ch-3 sp: [2 dc, ch 3, 2 dc] in ch-3 sp, work 1 dc in each of 21 dc along side of each motif, 1 dc in each ch sp where motifs adjoin, and 1 dc in sc at each join (the stitch used to join two motifs together); repeat from * 3 times. Join.

Joining front and back (color G)

Place front and back pieces right sides together and, starting at either top corner, join by working through both pieces together as follows: 2 sc in corner sp, [1 sc in each dc to bottom corner, (2 sc, ch 3, 2 sc) in corner sp] twice, 1 sc in each dc to top corner, 2 sc in corner sp. Fasten off and weave in ends.

Top trim (colors G and F)

This gives the bag a finishing touch and makes the opening more durable.

Round 1: Using color G and starting in any dc at top of bag: work 1 sc in each dc along front and back of bag, and 1 sc in each ch sp at sides of bag (the outer corners of front and back motifs at side seams). Join.

Round 2: Using color F and starting in any sc: work 1 sc in each sc around. Join.

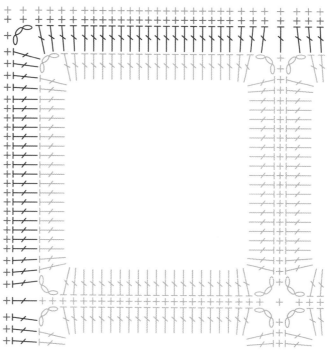

Border, joining front and back, and top trim

Bottom corner of bag for chart above

Strap rows 1–3;
repeat row 2 for
101 rows in total.

Strap (color F)

Row 1: Ch 8, 1 dc in third ch from
hook, 1 dc in each ch to end, turn.
Alternatively, crochet a row of
7 dc directly onto the side of
the bag.

Row 2: Ch 2 (counts as 1 dc),
1 dc in each st to end, turn.
(7 dc)

Repeat row 2 for length required.
You can make the strap as long as
you like; this one has 101 rows. Sew
the strap to the sides of the bag,
with the middle dc centered over
the seam between front and back
of bag.

LINING THE BAG

The cotton yarn, small hook, and solid crochet borders,
coupled with the dense multiple-loop petals, all help to
make this bag fairly robust. However, you could easily
line the bag with a pretty fabric if you wish. Cut out two
rectangles of fabric the same size as the bag, plus a little
extra as a seam allowance. With right sides together,
sew the two pieces of fabric together around three edges,
leaving the top open. Hem around the top. Insert the lining
into the bag with the right side facing inward and hand sew
the top of the lining to the inside of the bag. You could also
line the inside of the strap with matching fabric to make
that stronger too.

SKILL LEVEL: 🌼🌼

MOTIFS: 56 motifs, each 5½" (14cm) square

BLANKET: 40 x 46" (102 x 117cm)

Yarn

Bulky-weight bamboo/cotton yarn in 5 colors

A: gray 263yd (240m)

B: blue 263yd (240m)

C: pink 263yd (240m)

D: sand 328yd (300m)

E: off-white 1094yd (1000m)

Tools

Large circle loom

Crochet hook H/8 (5mm)

Yarn needle

Chart key

✳	fully sewn center
o	loom peg
⊙	ch
+	sc
⊥	dc
ⸯ	crab stitch

Vinni's Blanket

This blanket is made using a chunky bamboo/cotton yarn. The gorgeous softness of the yarn is echoed in the calm palette of pastel colors, together with off-white. The latter is repeated on the same rounds in each motif, enhancing the calmness of the color scheme. A simple border of crab stitch emphasizes the "squareness" of the blanket.

Pattern

Large circle loom (colors A–D)
Use each color to make the flowers for approx. 14 motifs; you don't have to make exactly the same number of flowers in each color, but keep in mind that you will need extra color D for the border. Wrap yarn 1 time around all 24 pegs. Cut yarn, leaving an extra long tail, and tie off at center back of flower.

Center (colors A–D)
Using long tail, secure bloom with a fully sewn center. Pop bloom off the loom and weave in ends.

Round 1 (color E)
Starting in any 2 petals and working through both loops together: *1 sc in 2 petals together, ch 4, [1 sc in next 2 petals together, ch 2] 2 times; repeat from * 3 times. Join.

Round 2 (color E)
Starting in any ch-4 sp: *[2 dc, ch 3, 2 dc] in ch-4 sp, [1 dc in next sc, 2 dc in ch-2 sp] 2 times, 1 dc in next sc; repeat from * 3 times. Join.

Round 3 (colors A–D)
Use a different color from the one used to make the flowers, combining pairs of colors at random. Starting in any corner ch-3 sp: *[2 dc, ch 3, 2 dc] in ch-3 sp, 1 dc in each of 11 dc; repeat from * 3 times. Join.

Round 4 (color E)
Starting in any corner ch-3 sp: *[2 sc, ch 2, 2 sc] in ch-3 sp, 1 sc in each of 15 dc; repeat from * 3 times. Join.

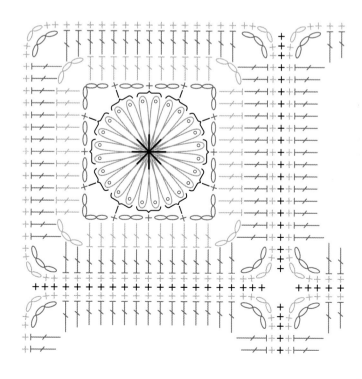

Joining motifs (color E)

Complete all motifs before joining. Lay them out so that all adjoining motifs have a different color combination for the flower and round 3. Place two motifs right sides together and join by working through both motifs together as follows: 1 sc in corner ch-1 sp, 1 sc through both loops of each sc along side, 1 sc in next corner ch-1 sp. Without cutting yarn, repeat to join the next two motifs. When the motifs are joined horizontally, repeat along the vertical sides. Weave in ends.

Border
Round 1 (color E)

Starting in any corner ch-2 sp: *[1 sc, ch 1, 1 sc] in ch-2 sp, work 1 sc in each sc along side of each motif, and 1 sc in each st where motifs adjoin (the stitch used to join two motifs together); repeat from * 3 times. Join.

Round 2 (color D)

Starting in any sc: work 1 crab stitch in each sc along sides and 2 crab stitches in each corner ch-1 sp around blanket; join. Also known as reverse single crochet, crab stitch is simply a single crochet stitch worked backward (from left to right instead of the usual right to left). To work a crab stitch, insert hook in next stitch to right of hook, yarn over and pull through stitch, yarn over and pull through both loops on hook. Weave in ends.

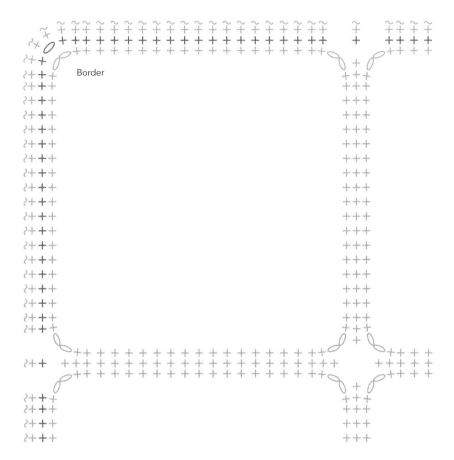

Border

TIP

I used a smaller crochet hook than usual for a bulky-weight yarn, but you could easily upsize to a size J/10 (6mm) hook if you would prefer a blanket with a looser drape. Remember that the finished blanket will be bigger and may require extra yarn if you do so.

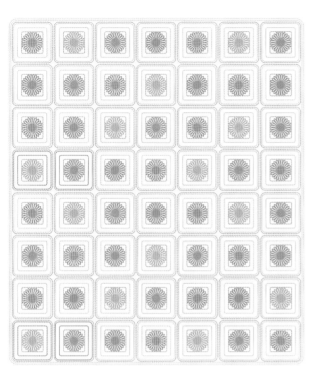

Arrange motifs in any
order you like, but try
to avoid joining motifs
that use the same color
combination for the
flower and round 3.

SKILL LEVEL:
MOTIFS: 24 motifs,
each 8" (20cm) diameter
THROW: 33 x 40"
(84 x 102cm)

Yarn

Super bulky-weight acrylic
yarn in 4 colors

A: dark gray 274yd (250m)

B: black 274yd (250m)

C: off-white 493yd (450m)

D: light gray 438yd (400m)

Tools

Two circle looms 4¾"
(12cm) and 2¾" (7cm)
diameter, each with
12 pegs (see page 127)

Crochet hook 12mm

Yarn needle

Chart key

✳ fully sewn
center

∘ loom peg

⬭ ch

+ sc

⊤ dc

Chunky Throw

Size does not have to be a limiting factor when flower looming. The
flowers of this throw have been upsized by using larger looms than for
the other motifs in this book. The super bulky but airy yarn is ideal for
making a practical, lightweight throw. A simple border lets the flowers
shine in all their fluffy glory.

Pattern

Larger circle loom (color A or B)
Use color A for half the motifs
and color B for the remainder.
Wrap yarn 2 times around all
12 pegs. Cut yarn, leaving an
extra long tail, and tie off at
center back of flower.

Smaller circle loom (color C)
Wrap yarn 1 time around all
12 pegs. Cut yarn and tie off
at center back of flower.

Center (color A or B)
Using long tail, secure bloom with
a fully sewn center. Pop bloom off
the loom and weave in ends.

Round 1 (color D)
Starting in any large petal and
working through lowest loop only
(1 loop remains loose): *1 sc in
each of 2 petals, ch 3; repeat from
* 5 times. Join.

Round 2 (color D)
Starting in first sc of any group
of 2 sc: *1 dc in each of 2 sc,
[2 dc, ch 2, 2 dc] in ch-3 sp;
repeat from * 5 times. Join.

Round 3 (color C)
Starting in any corner ch-2 sp:
*[1 sc, ch 1, 1 sc] in ch-2 sp, 1 sc
in each of next 6 dc; repeat from *
5 times. Join.

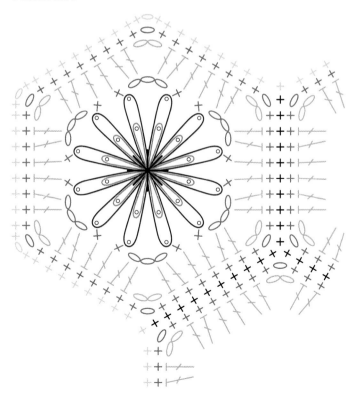

Joining motifs (color C)

Complete all motifs before joining. Place two motifs right sides together and join by working through both motifs together as follows: 1 sc in corner ch-1 sp, 1 sc through both loops of each sc along side, 1 sc in corner ch-1 sp. Without cutting yarn, repeat to join the next two motifs. When the motifs are joined horizontally, repeat along the vertical sides. Weave in ends.

Border (color C)

Starting in any outer corner ch-1 sp: work [1 sc, ch 1, 1 sc] in each ch-1 sp at outer corners, 1 sc in each sc along sides, and 1 sc in each sc at inner corners (the stitch used to join two motifs together). Weave in ends.

Making Your Own Flower Loom

The templates provided here will make a large circle and a large square flower loom, but can easily be resized.

Raid your recycling and you will find lots of materials for making flower looms—cardboard food or mail packaging or (clean) plastic food cartons, for example. Thick quilter's template plastic is another good (and more durable) option. The material needs to be rigid enough to hold its shape as you wrap the yarn, but flexible enough to allow you to ease the yarn loops off the tabs (use a yarn needle to flip them off).

Trace the template onto the loom material or hold a paper copy on top, and then cut out the shape using scissors or a craft knife. Be careful, but don't worry about being super accurate—yarn is a forgiving material. You may find it helpful to mark the top and bottom middle tabs. Make a small cut just to the right of the bottom tab and use this to anchor the starting end of the yarn.

If you want to make a long-lasting flower loom and have some woodworking skills, cut out the basic shape from wood. Hammer headless nails into the wood to form the pegs, or drill holes and insert wooden dowels. Saw a small notch for anchoring the yarn. I used a homemade wooden double loom (page 9) to make the Chunky Throw (page 124).

RESIZING

- Flower sizes may vary depending on the loom material, yarn, and wrapping tension, so always make a test motif to double-check sizes before embarking on a project.

- Small circle and square looms: Resize at 50%; omit alternate tabs, starting with tab next to a corner on square loom; lengthen tabs for more than 2–3 wraps.

- Medium circle loom: Resize at 70%; lengthen tabs for more than 3 wraps.

- Circle looms for Chunky Throw (page 124): Resize at 85% and 145%; omit alternate tabs.

- Resizing freehand: Draw a circle or square slightly smaller than the size of flower you wish to make. Then draw a slightly larger circle or square around it; this distance determines the length of the tabs. Mark the tabs, evenly spaced, between the two shapes. The width of the tabs will add a little extra length to the petals, so you will need to use trial and error if a precise flower size is required.

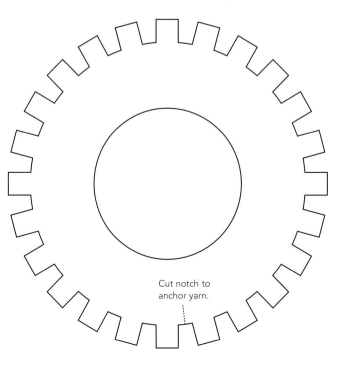

Cut notch to anchor yarn.

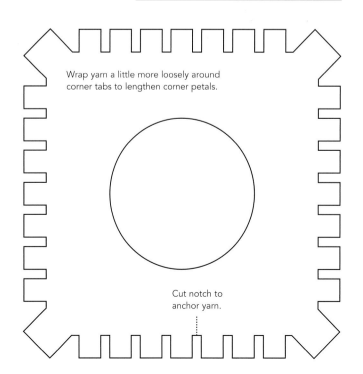

Wrap yarn a little more loosely around corner tabs to lengthen corner petals.

Cut notch to anchor yarn.

Index

Credits

Many thanks to Vinni's Colours and Scaapi for generously supplying Vinni's Nikkim yarn for all 30 motifs and Vinni's Tori yarn for Vinni's Blanket.

Vinni's Colours
www.vinniscolours.co.za
Tel: +27 (0)21 979 1629

Scaapi is a distributor of unique hand-dyed yarns.
www.scaapi.nl
info@scaapi.nl

All photographs and illustrations are the copyright of Quarto Publishing plc. While every effort has been made to credit contributors, Quarto would like to apologize should there have been any omissions or errors—and would be pleased to make the appropriate correction for future editions of the book.

Author's acknowledgments

A heartfelt thank you to all the lovely people at Quarto: Moira Clinch, Kate Kirby, Jackie Palmer, Michelle Pickering, Danielle Watt, and everybody else. Also a big thanks to Kuo Kang Chen for the amazing illustrations. It was truly wonderful to cooperate with you all on this new book and to explore together the best ways of introducing the craft of flower looming to readers. A last—but not least—thanks to you, the reader of this book…